W9-CKK-404

Profiting from Proliferation

DTBDC

•

Editor: Allen P. Webb

Practice Knowledge Manager: Catherine Wright
Managing Editor: Scott Leff
Editorial Production: Sue Catapano, Roger Draper, Karina Lacouture
Information Graphics: Mary Reddy
Art Director: Donald Bergh
Design and Layout: Veronica Belsuzarri, Delilah Zak

Illustrations by John Hersey, Roman Klonek, and Lloyd Miller

McKinsey & Company
55 East 52nd Street, New York, New York 10022
www.mckinseyquarterly.com

Profiting from Proliferation

McKinsey & Company

About this book

Eighteen months ago, my colleagues and I interviewed nearly 50 chief marketing officers from large companies in a variety of industries. We asked them about the most critical issues they faced. Overwhelmingly, the CMOs pointed to the challenges posed by the increased complexity of today's marketing environment: the growing fragmentation of customer segments, the simultaneous demand for both high- and low-end products and services, the declining effectiveness of traditional media, and the sheer number of touchpoints that customers now demand. The issue of complexity—or marketing proliferation, as we have come to call it—isn't new. But the CMOs felt that proliferation was becoming so severe that understanding its course and then evolving their strategies and organizations accordingly were of paramount importance.

That thirst for understanding and answers gave rise to this book. Its purpose is twofold: first, to provide an integrated picture of the most important activities required to generate profitable growth in a proliferating environment and, second, to share the lessons we have learned from our work with clients about how to make those changes happen. These objectives led us to synthesize the experiences of practitioners from around the world for our clients and colleagues rather than to develop our ideas in a book for mass distribution.

The breadth and depth of proliferation's impact are staggering. In industry after industry, the need to set priorities across exploding customer segments, channels, touchpoints, and media vehicles is challenging the brand, growth, sales, and service strategies of companies. Many marketers have spread their bets too thinly, thereby reducing the impact of their programs. Yet cutting off funding for some segments, channels, or media vehicles in order to free up resources for heavy investment in others is extremely risky in today's cluttered, competitive world. As a result, most marketers must improve the strategic integration of their resource allocation decisions dramatically.

Proliferation also poses challenges for the execution of marketing strategies—in particular, the ability to ensure the consistent delivery of brands across a number of touchpoints while keeping costs under control. Although marketing execution needs to be decentralized in a proliferating world, CMOs can't deliver the brand, product, or service experience their customers want, or the investment returns that CEOs and boards now demand, without a consistent approach to marketing and a coordinated performance-management system.

In fact, the need for profound changes in marketing strategy and for more consistent, efficient execution calls for a *commercial transformation*: "commercial" because the necessary changes will extend beyond the marketing organization, frequently requiring the CMO to lead ambitious cross-functional initiatives; "transformation" because adapting to a proliferating world will require fundamental changes in roles, responsibilities, processes, and capabilities.

Earlier this year, we shared a draft of this book with a group of executives and academics, including Gregory Lee, CMO of Samsung; Jim Stengel, CMO of P&G; Hans Straeberg, CEO of Electrolux; John Quelch, of the Harvard Business School; and Henrik Sattler, of the University of Hamburg. One observation they made was that while the scope of the proliferation challenge is as vast as we describe, different companies and industries will place different degrees of emphasis on the range of strategy and execution issues we discuss.

Consequently, we have tried to provide a number of options for reading this book. The table of contents provides a brief look at each chapter and highlights the book's four parts: the first chapter summarizes proliferation's current and expected future impact, three chapters outline the way marketing strategy must change in response, four chapters explore the necessary changes in marketing execution, and two final chapters discuss how to manage and lead a commercial transformation. We believe that the first and final chapters of the book will interest virtually all readers. Some will also want to read the middle two sections in their entirety; others can use the chapter summaries to choose what to read.

Although we hope that our thinking is both provocative and helpful, we don't believe that this book represents a final answer to the challenges of proliferation. So we are very interested in learning your reactions (which you can e-mail to us at proliferation@mckinsey.com) and hope that the book will initiate a dialogue with our readers on this topic, for which we collectively have such passion.

David C. Court
Director, Dallas office
McKinsey marketing and sales practice
March 2006

OVERVIEW

An explosion of new customer segments, sales and service channels, media, and brands is necessitating a transformation of marketing processes, roles, and capabilities. Companies need to become more sophisticated at prioritizing opportunities and allocating resources and increase the consistency and coordination of marketing execution.

STRATEGY

Launching new brands has never been easier—but sometimes less is more. With rigorous economic analysis and a deep understanding of customer preferences, marketers can clarify the competitive positioning of their brands, avoid offending the core customers of repositioned or discontinued ones, minimize cannibalization, and seize new opportunities.

To stimulate growth in today's marketing environment, companies must identify and prioritize opportunities at the points where proliferating segments, channels, and product categories intersect. A customer insights network helps marketers to look at the world through a number of lenses and to develop proprietary information about customers.

As sales and service interactions become increasingly important sources of competitive differentiation, more companies are getting stuck in the middle between low-frills and high-end competitors. Suppliers should segment customers according to their interaction requirements, build a *lean backbone* to meet shared needs, and establish affordable, high-touch overlays to satisfy more exacting demands.

EXECUTION

TRANSFORMATION

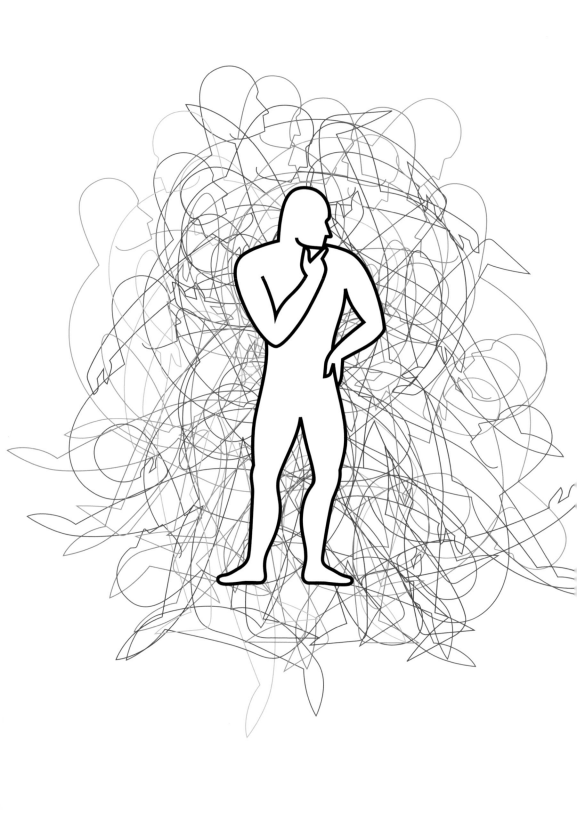

The proliferation challenge

**David C. Court, Thomas D. French, and
Trond Riiber Knudsen**

The scope of today's marketing challenge is breathtaking, and proliferation is the reason. Recent advances in technology, information, communications, and distribution have created an explosion of new customer
segments, sales and service channels, media, marketing approaches, products,
and brands. But despite better customer information management and lower
communications costs, marketing to consumers and businesses is becoming
more complex and difficult every day. Marketers—even the most sophisticated—are struggling to keep up.

To understand the full impact of proliferation, consider the wireless-
telecommunications market. Carriers used to manage 3 demographically
oriented consumer segments; today they manage more than 20 need- and
value-based ones. Rather than view baby boomers as a single segment, the
industry has created 6 or 8 subsegments, differentiated by their usage tendencies and product needs. The number of discrete offerings has ballooned
into the hundreds: prepaid and postpaid calling plans; family-friendly and
nights-and-weekend plans; text-, data-, and messaging-capable mobile
telephones; video and music phones; and so on. The number of distribution
touchpoints has increased from three to more than ten, including company-
owned stores, shared and exclusive dealers, telemarketing agents, affinity

partners, and the Web. As a result of customer-specific service bundles, the number of price points exceeds 500,000. And the number of communications vehicles will continue to grow dramatically as event marketing, viral marketing, product placement, and other approaches augment traditional media such as television, whose effectiveness is under assault.

The same picture holds true in business-to-consumer (B2C) and business-to-business (B2B) industries as varied as packaged goods, pharmaceuticals, retail banking, post and parcel, automotive, and advanced materials. Although proliferation is playing out differently across sectors, a few common characteristics underlie its challenge for marketers:

- *Polarizing and fragmenting customer segments.* In many industries, including cars, clothes, computers, and retailing, revenues are growing faster at the high and low ends of the market than in the middle (Exhibit 1). At the same time, in B2B markets such as air cargo and specialty chemicals, customers are becoming more discerning about when they are, and when they are not, willing to pay extra for premium offerings or solutions. For B2C and B2B companies alike, staying in the middle is often a death sentence, while focusing on just one end of the market is a recipe for slow or no growth.[1] What's more, in many B2C industries, marketers must contend with an increase in the number of meaningfully different customer segments—an increase resulting from factors such as the greater influence of ethnicity and lifestyle differences in consumption patterns.

EXHIBIT 1

The vanishing middle

Nominal growth of products, services in tier relative to market average for those products, services, 1999–2004, CAGR,[1] %

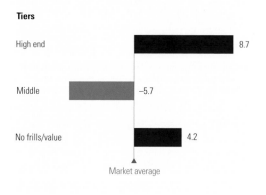

Tiers

High end 8.7

Middle –5.7

No frills/value 4.2

Market average

[1]25 industries or product categories—10 in Europe, 9 in North America, and 6 at global level; growth rate for each tier represents weighted average of industries and product categories studied; CAGR = compound annual growth rate.

---

[1]For more on market polarization, see Trond Riiber Knudsen, Andreas Randel, and Jørgen Rugholm, "The vanishing middle market," *The McKinsey Quarterly*, 2005 Number 4, pp. 6–9 (www.mckinseyquarterly.com/links/20906).

- *More sales and distribution touchpoints.* To meet the rising demand for convenience and flexibility, nearly all marketers are adding new channels, touchpoints, and, sometimes, distribution partners. By offering more sales and service options, marketers help consumers to cope with a busier, more complex world and enable B2B buyers to deal with an increasingly competitive environment. In so doing, these marketers have conditioned customers to expect great flexibility and choice. Even in an industry as basic as maintenance and repair operations, new technologies let companies offer more just-in-time channels, such as Internet ordering and on-site automatic parts dispensers. Yet the channel and touchpoint needs of customers vary widely by segment, and giving all of them everything they want is a recipe for financial ruin.

- *Diverse communications vehicles.* Advertising is exploding; in Germany, for example, the number of television commercials increased from 400,000 in 1991 to 2,500,000 a decade later. Cutting through such clutter is challenging and will become even more so. Rising advertising costs, an increasingly fragmented viewership, and the growing prominence of digital video recorders are reducing the efficacy of TV advertising, which by 2010, we estimate, could be only 35 percent as effective as it was in 1990. A similar story is playing out in direct marketing. For B2B marketing, the impact of recent trends is harder to measure but probably will be equally dramatic as media proliferation dampens the effectiveness of traditional vehicles, including sponsorship events and trade magazines.

  Alternative vehicles—such as the Internet, viral marketing, and product placement—show great promise: in some categories, banner ads and online video generate brand awareness more cost effectively than traditional television advertising. But these alternatives haven't achieved the scale needed to pick up the slack from traditional "workhorse" communications vehicles. Advertising will thus be effective only if marketers can manage a diverse and complex media mix.

Marketers have responded to proliferation by bolting on new brands, new customer segment strategies and segment managers, new-channel program managers, and, most recently, new strategies for evolving communications vehicles, such as the Web and viral marketing. These responses are not only adding to costs but also introducing a host of problems, including lower customer satisfaction resulting from inconsistencies across channels and segments, a lower level of insight into the needs of customers as each new team focuses on executing its own piece of the marketing program, and a decrease in agility as the organization as a whole responds more slowly to changes in the competitive landscape and the marketplace.

Dealing with—indeed, profiting from—proliferation calls for a more complete solution that requires a fundamental reassessment of marketing strategy, execution, and organization. As the marketing environment fragments, companies need to become more sophisticated at identifying, prioritizing, and allocating resources toward the most attractive segment and channel opportunities. Many marketers will thus have to overhaul their brand, growth, and sales and service strategies. To avoid mushrooming complexity and to keep from dissipating economies of scale while pursuing growth amid proliferation, the marketing organization will also need to increase its consistency and its coordination of execution dramatically in areas such as pricing, segment management, and promotional spending. It all adds up to an unprecedented level of change for marketers: a true transformation of processes, roles, and capabilities.

Proliferation and marketing strategy

In an environment of proliferation, a marketer's capacity to generate profitable growth depends on the ability to recognize and invest resources in opportunities lying at the intersection of ever-expanding numbers of customer segments, distribution channels, and product categories.

Frequently, though, the results of such efforts disappoint. Although many marketers are launching new brands or subbrands to address their customers' fragmented needs, they often achieve little revenue growth and suffer from increased complexity and diminished brand power. Others provide a wide variety of sales and service touchpoints but are becoming vulnerable to attack because their basic transaction costs are too high to compete with no-frills specialists and they lack the sophistication to take on high-end solutions specialists. In many industries, such as retail banking (Exhibit 2), the satisfaction of customers actually declines as they struggle to navigate the channels available to them.

These issues may sound disconnected, but they all reflect a common strategic problem: isolated, poorly integrated responses to proliferation inhibit companies from identifying the most valuable opportunities and from

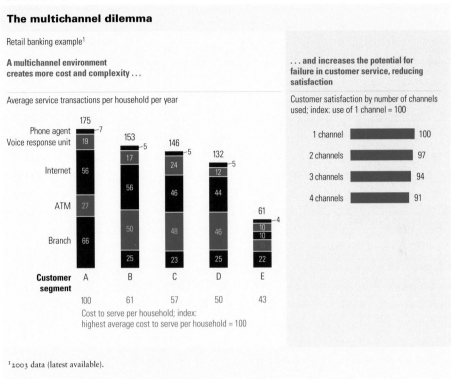

EXHIBIT 2

The multichannel dilemma

Retail banking example[1]

A multichannel environment creates more cost and complexity ...

Average service transactions per household per year

... and increases the potential for failure in customer service, reducing satisfaction

Customer satisfaction by number of channels used; index: use of 1 channel = 100

[1]2003 data (latest available).

allocating the human and financial resources needed to seize them cost effectively. Only with greater integration of brand, growth, sales, and service strategies can companies respond coherently to the challenge of proliferation.

Brand strategy

An explosion of brands in industries such as autos, pharmaceuticals, and white goods is leading companies toward brand strategies at either of two extremes: trying to have just one brand for each growth opportunity or shifting to a megabrand whose breadth frequently makes it difficult to reach customers.

The right way to set brand strategy in a proliferating environment is to spend less time on individual brand activities and more on making decisions about the portfolio as a whole. Successful portfolio approaches require companies to prune some brands and to identify strong ones that can be stretched into adjacent spaces crossing the lines of segments or business units: consider

P&G's phaseout of more than 1,000 brands over the past half dozen years and IBM's successful stretch of its core brand from hardware to services. Active portfolio management that establishes roles, relationships, and boundaries between brands is critical to getting brand strategy right on an ongoing basis.

Growth strategy

In today's marketing environment, strategies for stimulating growth depend heavily on insights about the preferences and behavior of customers at the points where segments, channels, and categories intersect. Centralized market research groups cannot dig deeply enough at those intersection points to obtain valuable data, to create true insights by integrating this information, or to transform insights into channel-, category-, or format-specific activities.

Marketers need an *insights network* whose interconnecting parts include data from many internal and external sources that, when integrated, can yield a proprietary edge, as well as partners that can provide and help analyze some of the needed data. Leading credit card companies, such as American Express and Capital One, buy external customer data, merge this information with existing databases on credit card usage, and develop rich customer profiles. High-powered insights networks also incorporate innovative qualitative or experiential research to improve the company's understanding of the customer. One example is the in-context interviews that some pharmaceutical companies use to gather breakthrough insights into what the industry calls "noncompliance"—the failure of patients to take the medications prescribed for them. To ensure that insights generated by the network help companies prioritize their opportunities, they must embed those insights in their key decisions by restructuring processes for brand and sales planning, new-product development, and marketing investments.

Sales and service strategy

Even as companies in many industries add channels, they endure declining customer satisfaction plus competitive attacks from low-cost specialists and high-end solutions players. Why? Those companies are allocating sales and service resources relatively uniformly, with each account and channel receiving resources proportionate to its size, regardless of how customers want to interact with their sales or service provider or how profitable they may be. Such an approach is problematic in an environment of proliferating distribution channels, which make it easy for customers to mix and match suppliers.

Companies must redefine how they allocate sales and service resources.

Their first step should be to determine what level of support their customers need for each type of interaction—by assessing, for example, the preferences of customers and their willingness to pay for in-person versus telephone-based help for basic service problems or sales calls. For interactions that cut across all customers, companies need a high-quality, low-cost platform for sales support and service processes. This *lean backbone* typically includes hotlines for customers, order-processing systems, and central sales-support functions (such as frequently used sales materials) that companies employ repeatedly. It's also necessary to develop customized modules, or high-touch overlays, when customers value additional sales or service support enough to cover its cost (Exhibit 3). These modules might include teams of industry experts, solutions-development teams, and "hunting" teams that focus on acquiring new customers. The result is a more selective response to fragmenting customer needs and to proliferating sales and service touchpoints.

Proliferation and marketing execution

These new strategies require well-coordinated execution that delivers consistent, cost-effective marketing programs for the segments, channels, formats, and categories where companies are seeking growth. At many companies, though, proliferation is breeding inconsistency, as the managers added to ensure the right focus on new segments or channels build their own Web sites, hire their own advertising agencies, develop their own

EXHIBIT 3

Mix it up

Interaction variables per customer segment

		Customer segment			
		A	B	C	D
High-touch overlays	Key accounts		●	●	●
Customized service modules for customers who are willing to pay for additional sales/service	Vertical specialists				●
	Dedicated inside sales			●	●
	Transactional face-to-face sales	●			
Lean backbone	Sales support	●	●	●	●
A high-quality, low-cost platform of sales support and customer service processes	Call center	●	●	●	●
	Web site	●	●	●	●

variants on the company's brand positioning, and establish their own measurement systems. The consequences include rising costs, complexity, and customer confusion. In addition, senior marketing executives, such as CMOs and global brand managers, are frustrated to find that they can't quickly obtain comparable information about financial performance, customer satisfaction, or brand health across business units, regions, channels, and segments.

To be sure, superb marketing in today's environment calls for decentralized segment and channel management. Yet neither uncoordinated decentralization nor bureaucratic centralization is sufficient on its own to cope with proliferation. What's required is more of a clean-sheet approach that defines "how we do marketing," which in turn drives systems, processes, templates, tools, and performance-management techniques across key segments and channels. The end result is far more than a loose set of guidelines; it's a true *commercial operating system* that helps stamp out unjustified internal complexity, ensures that best practices are shared quickly, and supports speedy reactions to marketplace changes. Marketers need this kind of consistency and coordination to deal with the execution challenges that proliferation poses in managing brands, key accounts, marketing investments, pricing, and segmentation. Three examples will help illustrate the benefits.

Consistency in pricing

Companies must now juggle thousands—in some cases, millions—of price points while seeking to maintain a consistent pricing and communications strategy across an ever-increasing number of products and vehicles. Even companies that use state-of-the-art approaches to analyze and improve their pricing performance are frequently disappointed with the results. The reason is that traditional management approaches, which distribute responsibility for pricing decisions across functions and geographies, are inadequate in today's complex environment.

Proliferation therefore demands a new approach to pricing, with highly transparent processes and performance standards; a common system for pricing across brands, channels, and segments; and organizational balance achieved through a central pricing group that integrates the model throughout the company but doesn't make every decision. In many cases, this new approach will require substantial changes in the way companies make their daily pricing decisions, as well as revised systems, organizational roles and responsibilities, performance metrics, and incentives.

Consistency in customer segment management

Since market polarization and proliferating distribution channels have made customer segments more fluid and shifts in value among them more common, managing segments has assumed greater importance. Advances in customer relationship management (CRM) and other technologies have helped marketers to keep customer-level scorecards and to consolidate them on a timely basis. Even so, bolt-on management approaches and functional silos prevent many companies from consistently measuring, understanding, and focusing management attention on what happens within and across segments—to say nothing of how these developments relate to aggregate marketing plans.

To realize the benefits of a focus on changes occurring within and across segments, companies must fully integrate segment planning and performance management with their traditional business-planning process. The typical organization can begin to accomplish this goal through segment-oriented performance measurement and reporting. Over time, the company is likely to need segment owners. Although they can augment rather than replace the organization's existing product, service, and functional units, they must have meaningful influence over the allocation of resources related to segment-level targets and be accountable for identifying and delivering distinctive value to the most attractive customer segments.

Consistency in managing marketing investments

A third area where more consistent operating practices are particularly valuable is helping companies to improve their marketing ROI—the returns they earn on their marketing investments. Media fragmentation and the declining efficacy of traditional television ads are undermining those returns and making it more difficult than ever to measure them.

At a time of splintering audiences and media, marketers can create a coherent overview of a company's entire marketing outlay by consistently applying investment fundamentals, such as clarifying the objectives of marketing investments, finding and exploiting points of economic leverage in the business, managing risk, and creating greater transparency about the profitability of marketing programs across business units. Following these principles while applying increasingly sophisticated, well-proven analytic tools also helps marketers to intervene at the specific points of economic leverage where the returns on investment are highest. In this way, marketers can mitigate the dilutive effect of a fragmenting environment in which most new vehicles (such as the Internet, viral marketing, product placement, and cell phones) remain below scale.

Managing the commercial transformation

The level of change required to profit from proliferation involves what we refer to as a *commercial transformation*—an overhaul of a company's core marketing and sales processes, roles, and capabilities.

Carrying off change of this magnitude at a brisk pace is difficult in any functional area, and several factors make it particularly tricky in marketing. Marketing and sales organizations are more diverse and complex than the shop floors where many improvement programs take place, so it's tough to keep disparate parts of the organization working together. Furthermore, since jump-starting growth is often the rationale for a commercial transformation, the effort requires not just strong execution but also creativity—which raises the degree of difficulty and the complexity of the decision making. Finally, uncertainty in predicting the responses of competitors and customers to marketing changes makes it challenging to eliminate variability (a goal of many operational-change efforts), places a premium on flexibility, and complicates the establishment of goals and metrics.

As a result, executives orchestrating wholesale change in sales and marketing organizations need to take several steps that go beyond traditional change-management techniques. First, they should not only set aspirations bold enough to require better integration of far-flung parts of the organization but also lead the transformation more forcefully than they might think necessary. Second, they should particularly emphasize building new skills, changing mind-sets, and establishing new ways of working. These efforts often take place in the context of installing a new commercial operating system, which can serve as a way to catalyze change and then institutionalize it. Third, senior executives will have to make trade-offs—such as how centralized the effort should be and how much they should tailor it to the needs of individual business units—more frequently and in greater detail than they do in most operational-change programs. If executives instead allow business units, countries, and districts to choose from a broad menu of ideas and tools, the transformation will probably fail.

These issues aren't just for CMOs and senior marketing executives. Given the far-reaching nature of the changes that proliferation requires, CEOs too must be involved in the transformation. Without their participation, it's difficult to have what P&G's CEO, Alan G. Lafley, says are the elements critical to an effective transformation: "disciplined strategic choices, structure that supports the strategy, systems that enable large organizations to work and execute together, winning culture, and leadership."

The rewards—profitable growth and sustainable differentiation against companies that don't overhaul their marketing model—make the effort worthwhile. The future will belong to companies that capture the fragmented opportunities that proliferation presents while maintaining consistency, coordination, and scale.

David Court (david_court@mckinsey.com), **Tom French** (tom_french@mckinsey.com), and **Trond Riiber Knudsen** (trond_riiber_knudsen@mckinsey.com) are members of McKinsey's global marketing and sales practice. David Court is a director in McKinsey's Dallas office, Tom French is a director in the Boston office, and Trond Riiber Knudsen is a director in the Oslo office.

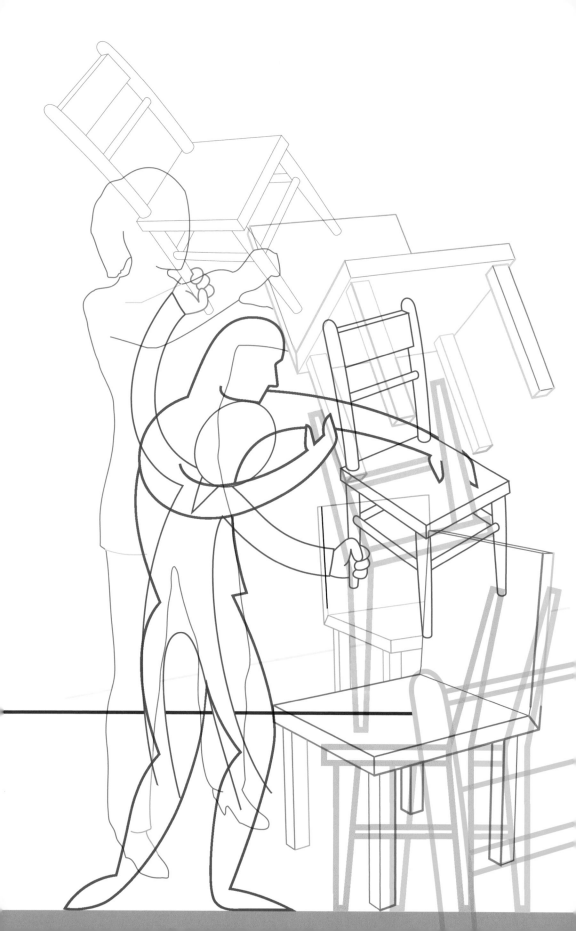

Designing and managing winning brand portfolios

Stephen J. Carlotti Jr., Mary Ellen Coe, and Jeskó Perrey

In today's proliferating marketing environment, it is more important than ever to manage brands as a portfolio. Most companies, though, undermanage their portfolios. One reason is historical: this approach was less relevant when entrepreneurial brand managers were initially building the world's great brands. Also, it's challenging to craft an effective portfolio strategy and to align the organization behind one.

While weak portfolio management is a perennial issue, it has become more significant as several forces work in favor of launching new brands: customer segments are multiplying, distribution and certain communication costs are falling, and manufacturing flexibility is on the rise. When we factor in the heavy pressure on marketers to produce growth, it comes as little surprise that brands (including subbrands and line extensions) have been proliferating at a breakneck pace in industries such as beverages, consumer durables, food, household goods, and pharmaceuticals.[1]

More hasn't always been better. Some of the new brands have lacked scale and sufficient strength to increase revenues. In confectionery, for

---

[1] Roughly three-quarters of the Fortune 1000 consumer goods companies manage more than 100 brands each. From 1997 to 2001, the number of brands increased by 79 percent in the pharmaceutical industry, by 60 percent in white goods and travel and leisure, by 46 percent in the automotive industry, and by at least 15 percent in food, household goods, and beverages.

EXHIBIT I

Not so sweet

Confectionery sector example

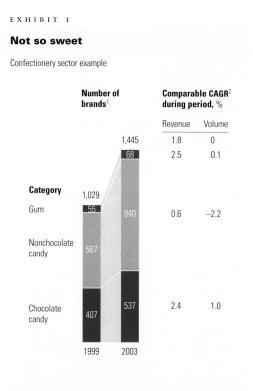

	Number of brands[1]		Comparable CAGR[2] during period, %	
			Revenue	Volume
		1,445	1.8	0
		68	2.5	0.1
Category	1,029			
Gum	55	840	0.6	−2.2
Nonchocolate candy	567			
Chocolate candy	407	537	2.4	1.0
	1999	2003		

[1]Includes subbrands and major product variants; excludes brands with <0.1% share of revenues within respective category.
[2]Compound annual growth rate.

Source: Information Resources, Inc. (IRI); McKinsey analysis

example, the number of brands increased by more than 40 percent in recent years, but overall revenue and volume haven't kept pace (Exhibit 1). Most individual candy brands have a smaller market share than they did a few years ago. Furthermore, brand proliferation imposes significant costs. These stem from the added complexity of managing a portfolio of brands across the product life cycle, which in turn fragments company resources, creates diseconomies of scale, and diminishes brand power.

To translate the proliferation of brand opportunities into profitable growth, companies need a customer-based portfolio strategy that balances economic opportunity with realistic estimations of brand equity. At a minimum, such a strategy will yield clearer roles, relationships, and boundaries for brands, and let them more effectively target discrete channel and segment opportunities. In many cases, the result will be a stable of fewer, more powerful brands. Since new portfolio strategies frequently prompt competitive responses and have unanticipated consequences, companies also will have to change the organization to facilitate quick, coordinated responses for the portfolio as a whole and for individual brands. Robust metrics that highlight unexpected shifts enable a coherent response.

Some leading marketers already are placing heightened emphasis on portfolio management. Anheuser-Busch uses a coordinated approach: it recognizes that customers shift to different beers (from lower- to higher-end or fuller to lighter brews, for example), and its portfolio strategy aims to keep those customers within its family of brands when they do so. P&G and Unilever recently have phased out many brands (P&G more than 1,000 over the past half dozen years). Several other consumer goods companies have achieved rates of revenue growth two to five times higher than their historic norms and saved 20 percent of their overall marketing expenditures by managing their brand portfolios more effectively. Given the historic and organizational forces favoring single-brand management, such results are possible only when senior executives take active responsibility for the portfolio as a whole.

The temptation to brand

In addition to meeting the perennial need for growth, marketers have been launching more brands in response to the fragmentation of traditional segments. Consider, for example, how customers are migrating out of the middle to the low and high ends of the market in cars, clothes, computers, retailing, and other industries.[2] At the same time, while globalizing consumer tastes are creating segments in some markets that cut across geographies, growing ethnic diversity in other markets is exacerbating fragmentation as customers seek products with local flavor.

Furthermore, it's increasingly feasible for marketers to develop and launch brands cost-effectively for fragmenting customer segments. Distribution costs and communication costs are falling, and manufacturing flexibility is on the rise.

Distribution costs

To get an idea of how falling costs of distribution encourage marketers to launch new brands, consider two very different industries: automobile insurance and bottled water. For auto insurers, new channels such as the Internet have lowered customer acquisition costs for new brands, making their launch more economical. In bottled water, consolidation in the retail channel has reduced the number of negotiations required to reach critical mass and, thus, lowered the barriers to brand entry.

Communication costs

The cost of reaching consumers also has declined in some situations. For example, evidence suggests that digital media such as banner ads, paid search, and online video can be more cost effective than traditional media,

---

[2] For more on market polarization, see Trond Riiber Knudsen, Andreas Randel, and Jørgen Rugholm, "The vanishing middle market," *The McKinsey Quarterly*, 2005 Number 4, pp. 6–9 (www.mckinseyquarterly.com/links/20906).

such as print, telemarketing, and television. When marketers incorporate effective viral distribution techniques, they could further increase cost savings. As a result, small budgets—carefully targeted and often heavily concentrated in digital media—have successfully launched brands such as eBay, Firefox (the Internet browser), Google, and Red Bull.

Production flexibility

Finally, increasingly flexible manufacturing processes have made it economical to create more product variations, thereby reducing barriers to entry for new brands and products. For example, Toyota Motor now has five SUV models in North America, (4Runner, Highlander, Land Cruiser, RAV4, and Sequoia), where the company used to have two.

The downside

Launching new brands looks more important and economical than ever, at least on the face of it. As brands proliferate, however, complexity costs lead to a more unwieldy brand portfolio—one in which weaker brands labor to connect with consumers—and to diseconomies of scale.

Complexity

An ever-growing number of brands imposes complexity costs along each brand's entire life cycle, from product development and sourcing (more R&D resources) to manufacturing and distribution (more labor schedules to coordinate) to sales and channel management (more training and more brands than the sales force can really focus on) to marketing and promotions (more documentation and more coordination of marketing vendors and agencies). A key part of this complexity is difficulty establishing and maintaining the boundaries between brands, a task that becomes more challenging with each new brand in the portfolio and with each new country served. (One rationale for Unilever's brand rationalization was the cross-border-management challenge of maintaining about 20 margarine brands throughout Europe.)

Diminished brand power

As companies add more and more brands to the portfolio, they have greater difficulty developing and supporting truly distinctive brands. Instead, the portfolio consists of many smaller brands that lack enough users and word-of-mouth equity to achieve the iconic status that characterizes powerful brands. This is partly due to the budget constraints of an overly broad portfolio: brands suffer from insufficient funding to support advertising, for example, or new product innovation. Since all brands are looking to innovate, there are clearly risks that innovation resources will be spread too thinly to support any one brand.

As Sony has introduced new products, it has moved away from using the Sony brand name. Therefore, Sony subbrands such as PlayStation and the recently discontinued Qualia are associated primarily with the products they support and have limited common connection to the iconic Sony brand. Not only has this diminished the ability to leverage subbrands, including PlayStation, in other product areas, but the power of the Sony brand as a whole is no longer reinforced through the product offerings.

Launch and support diseconomies

Finally, a more complex brand portfolio reduces economies of scale, particularly around the launch of a new product or service and in the ongoing support of that product or service. The more brands that exist within a portfolio, the greater will be the tendency to spread support across brands rather than concentrating it on a particular brand or platform. Furthermore, ongoing brand support becomes more complex as brands compete for a generally fixed pool of resources. As a consequence, every brand has to share, and the strongest brands are often underresourced as focus is diffused across many, smaller brands.

Crafting a portfolio strategy

To deal with the rising cost of complexity, companies need a flexible portfolio approach that is sensitive to consumers and current brands alike. While bold, top-down declarations of intent do have a place, marketers will be better served by first clarifying the needs that brands could satisfy and then assessing both the economic attractiveness of meeting them and their fit with the positioning of existing brands. Only then should marketers move to increase the portfolio's value by making strategic decisions on the restructuring, acquisition, divestiture, or launch of brands.

Start with the consumer

The starting point for marketers is to define categories as consumers do. Over the past decade or so, PepsiCo has recognized that customers choose among all nonalcoholic beverages, not just carbonated ones, to satisfy their

EXHIBIT 2

What they want and how they want it

Customer 'need states' (processed-foods example)

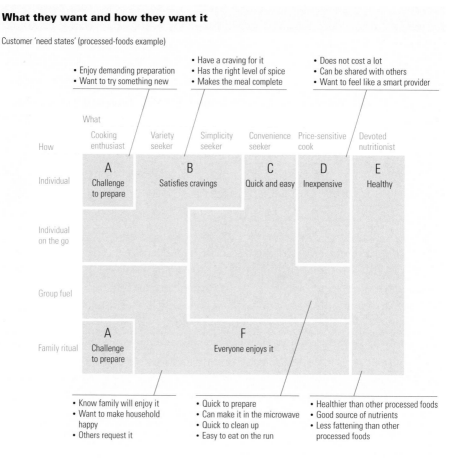

need for refreshment. It has therefore made acquisitions (Gatorade, SoBe, Tropicana), developed new products (Amp, Aquafina), and completed several joint ventures (the one with Starbucks led to bottled Frappuccino). Strong operating results have followed.[3]

Successes such as PepsiCo's—as well as Kellogg's winning move from breakfasts to nutritional minimeals and P&G's repositioning of Olay from moisturizing products to all skin- and beauty-care offerings—result from a judicious, deliberate broadening of a company's frame of reference. The revised view of consumer needs is neither too narrow and category

---

[3] Pepsi's share of the US noncarbonated segment increased from 37.6 percent in 2000 to 45.6 percent in 2003. At the same time, Coca-Cola's share increased to 28.4 percent, from 25.3 percent. These figures exclude Tropicana's 100 percent fruit juice products. Had they been included, Pepsi's lead over Coke would be even greater. Pepsi has the number-one brand in water, juices, iced tea, and sports drinks.

constrained nor too broad and conceptual. Moving gradually often helps companies strike such a balance; PepsiCo, for instance, initially expanded its frame of reference from cola drinks to all carbonated beverages and only later moved into nonalcoholic, nondairy ones. The fit between the redefined frame of reference and existing organizational capabilities also provides a reality check. When an expanded frame of reference implies brand extension opportunities that a company can't easily seize by itself, it must weigh the benefits of acquisitions or partnerships to broaden its portfolio against their complexity costs.

Within a given frame of reference, marketers need a disciplined way of evaluating their brands' opportunities. One is to scrutinize *need states*— the intersection between what customers want and how they want it (Exhibit 2). Many marketers think about need states from time to time, but most define their brands by product (for instance, an economy brand) or consumer segment (young adults, say) instead of consumer needs ("people consume this brand when they want something cheap, don't care about nutrition, and can't spend time cooking at home"). Although thinking through need states is demanding, it often suggests new ways for existing brands to satisfy the needs of customers, thereby helping marketers avoid the common trap of launching a new brand every time they want to enter a market.

When a global brewer scrutinized the need states of its customers, it discovered that there was no single "import" segment; a wide range of people bought imports across several need states. Such findings show that the approach of offering one brand per customer segment can be mistaken. If the occasions when consumers use a product largely shape their needs, it is often appropriate to offer the target consumer a number of brands.

Balance economic opportunity with brand reality

Need states are more than descriptive tools; they also represent market opportunities. To evaluate them, marketers must begin by estimating their size. Since need states rarely coincide with conventional market definitions, marketers often must creatively piece together known data on segment share and channel mix. Category, consumer, product, and packaging trends can point to the likely future size of need states, and potential shifts in the intensity of competition can shed light on future profitability. The resulting profit pool map (Exhibit 3, on the next spread) reveals attractive opportunities for brands to target.

But make no mistake: a profit map is no portfolio strategy. For starters, to target some seemingly attractive need states, the company may have to reposition brands so much that they no longer appeal to their original consumers. Such considerations help explain Toyota Motor's 1989 decision to launch Lexus as a separate brand and not as a new Toyota model. By contrast, Mazda Motor's much-praised Millenia luxury car struggled with its brand identity from introduction in 1994 until it was phased out in 2003.

To avoid positioning mistakes, marketers must understand each brand's unique contribution to the portfolio. A helpful starting point is to map the company's current brands against the universe of relevant need states. Marketers should use statistical tools and market research to assess the relationship between the things customers value in a given need state and the attributes that differentiate the brand for them.[4] By combining this consumer knowledge with conventional metrics (such as each brand's market share within a variety of need states, as well as the proportion of each brand's volume that a need state represents), marketers can see the attainable opportunities for each brand and the amount of differentiation or overlap within the portfolio.

Many companies mapping out their portfolios find they have at least one relatively weak brand. Some choose to retain and improve underperformers rather than jettisoning them or targeting them toward new customers, but that approach carries risks. Frequently, companies that hold on to underperformers can't really support all of their brands, so they have to make small cuts in the resources allotted to each, thereby undermining the performance of their portfolios. One benefit of developing a profit map is that it helps catalyze more dramatic action by painting a clear picture of the economic opportunities that companies forgo if they don't take the portfolio approach.

Make the tough choices

Marketers generally have two options for achieving their portfolio goals. First, they can restructure their brands by repositioning those that have lost relevance to the target segments, by consolidating two or more mature brands competing for the same consumers, or by divesting a brand that absorbs more resources than it contributes and holds little promise of a turnaround. Restructuring doesn't involve pursuing customers whom a company doesn't currently serve; rather, it means changing the brands that serve its present customers. The other option is to change the portfolio to

---

[4] Such an analysis is also frequently the starting point for efforts to set individual brand strategies. In fact, the mapping of brands against need states represents the intersection of portfolio and single-brand strategies. For more on individual brand strategies and statistical tools, see Nora A. Aufreiter, David Elzinga, and Jonathan W. Gordon, "Better branding," *The McKinsey Quarterly*, 2003 Number 4, pp. 28–39 (www.mckinseyquarterly.com/links/21112).

drive new growth by launching a new brand, acquiring or licensing one from another company, or redefining an existing brand to target a new category of customers.

Restructuring is scary because it involves modifying brands and consumer attitudes. But though careful management is certainly needed to restructure brands without losing customers, the risk of adding new brands or categories is often greater—and so are the investments. Value-creating brand acquisitions are few and far between. Roughly three-quarters of all new brands fail. And despite success stories such as P&G's recent expansion of the Mr. Proper brand in Germany from a floor-cleaning agent into a detergent, stretching brands into any new category is risky because it's easy to go too far and lose their identity. Brand managers are accustomed to making headlines through launches or acquisitions, but those tactics are usually the last to consider for a portfolio strategy.

Of course, companies can rework their brand portfolios in a number of ways, which are often interconnected (repositioning of one brand may have

EXHIBIT 3

Pools of profit

Share of total profits by customer 'need state' (processed-foods example)

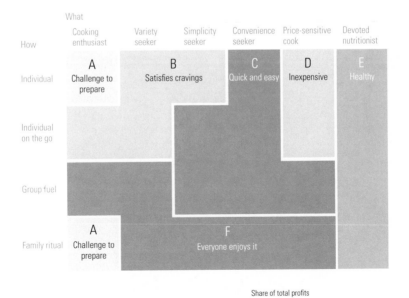

ripple effects for others), so it isn't practical to evaluate each brand move in isolation. Marketers must therefore develop and compare a manageable number of plausible scenarios that bundle compatible moves. Each scenario should involve only a few moves (Exhibit 4); more than four or five can overwhelm a marketing organization and confuse consumers. To define those moves, a company must make decisions about issues such as the right number of brands—and which to have—and the advisability of offering umbrella brands with subbrands rather than a medley of individual brands.

Several rules of thumb help marketers avoid playing a trial-and-error game. First, they can build their strategies around leading brands. If well-known ones are financially successful, their role in the portfolio shouldn't change much, but when they underperform, it's critical to adjust their positioning before recrafting the roles of other brands. Second, marketers must ensure that their sophisticated and ambitious portfolio ideas are feasible in view of internal resource constraints and likely competitive reactions. Finally, they should know when a brand is the consumer's second choice. Research techniques such as conjoint analysis can help them learn whether two or more adjacent brands are taking share and margins from each other or from competitors.

For an international industrial-equipment manufacturer, building the portfolio around a leading global brand has been a straightforward affair in many markets but problematic where the company's other brands are powerful leaders. In those countries, the company makes styling adjustments and includes features valued locally even though they increase the complexity of its offerings. It also found that in some markets, it sold similar products at different prices. The resulting cannibalization—people usually bought the cheaper offering—was costly. By clarifying brand roles, making local adjustments when necessary, and doubling the number of shared parts in products, the manufacturer raised its portfolio sales by 3 percent in a stagnant market and cut its development costs by up to 5 percent.

Managing the portfolio

Getting strategy right is only part of the battle; companies also must improve their ability to manage brand portfolios if they are to adapt quickly to shifting trends, competitive responses, mergers, and new-product launches while also paying heed to the natural life cycle of their brands. Since taking action with one often means doing so with another, companies must determine, on an ongoing basis, how well individual brands are fulfilling their part in the portfolio strategy and whether the strategy itself still makes sense.

EXHIBIT 4

Brand scenarios

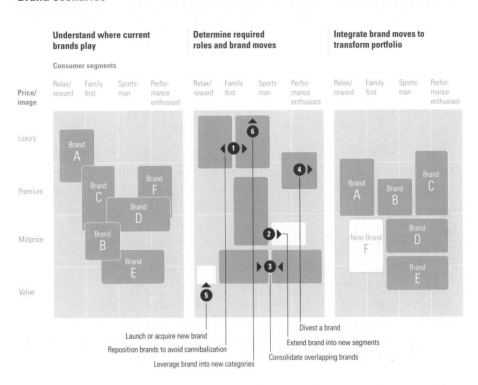

| | Understand where current brands play | Determine required roles and brand moves | Integrate brand moves to transform portfolio |

Consumer segments

Launch or acquire new brand

Reposition brands to avoid cannibalization

Leverage brand into new categories

Consolidate overlapping brands

Extend brand into new segments

Divest a brand

Sometimes the chief marketing officer, vice president for marketing, or a person who rose through the ranks of the marketing organization and then became general manager of a business unit can oversee portfolio management while still carrying out his or her primary duties. The support team might consist primarily of swing analysts who have some responsibility for individual brands but can be called upon for major events, such as a new-product launch or the acquisition of several brands. At the extreme, brand teams might have a fluid membership. In other cases—particularly in industries characterized by rapidly changing tastes (fashion), many subbrands (autos), or rapid consolidation—a full-time portfolio-management structure may be warranted.

Whatever structure a company selects, senior executives need unity of purpose across functions and businesses and robust metrics for tracking performance if they are to channel the entrepreneurial energies of the brand managers in the right direction and, when necessary, make them trim their sails or change course.

Building alignment that supports the portfolio

For starters, companies need a common language and approach for communicating about the roles and boundaries of each brand in the portfolio. Many companies talk of business or investment roles with terms such as "grow," "sustain," and "milk," but these aren't relevant to the brand portfolio strategy. In contrast, well-defined portfolio roles include the target customer for the brand, the brand's goal with the target (such as trial or loyalty), and the boundary conditions on the brand with respect to product range, price, promotions, and places where the brand can be sold. Communicating in these ways helps companies clarify and sustain boundaries between brands while avoiding counterproductive tactics.

Senior executives also must reconcile the portfolio strategy with functional agendas elsewhere in the company. They might, for example, determine they should set up focused R&D initiatives to fill gaps in the brand portfolio, work with the finance organization to include key brand metrics in annual and long-range plans, and have the sales organization develop a calendar and guidelines for resource allocation. The calendar would be linked to key dates in the strategy's rollout, and the guidelines would include directions for presenting brands to intermediaries such as grocery stores or car dealers.

Tracking progress

Many companies underemphasize the next crucial task: measuring whether each brand is fulfilling its role in the portfolio while operating within agreed-upon boundary conditions. Typically, two types of metrics are important. First, to facilitate cross-brand comparisons, marketers need standard measures of volume, growth, and consumer behavior—such as whether consumers know about, have tried, or ever considered purchasing a brand; their attitudes toward it (for instance, is it "worth paying more for"?); rates for converting prospects into customers and for retaining customers in target segments; percentage considering the brand a second choice; and levels of customer satisfaction. Second, marketers should add metrics that are tailored to the strategic goals for each brand. If the managers of several brands in the same portfolio track only identical metrics, the company often has a problem. Either the metrics are at too high a level to shed light on the performance of different brands, or the brands are positioned so closely together that the strategy needs rethinking.

An appliance maker introducing a new, lower-priced line to its portfolio benefited from tracking product mix changes by sales channels. It discovered that in some channels, its existing premium products were positioned close to the new line, a problem that leads to cannibalization and falling margins. The timely channel data prompted the company to stop the bleeding quickly. Well-conceived metrics also clarify major competitive moves. In the value end of the appliance industry, LG Electronics and Samsung have made advances that are prompting several other manufacturers to rethink the role of value offerings in their own portfolios.

Although the annual planning process is a natural time for such dialogues, brand managers should raise red flags whenever these issues appear, particularly if the likely response includes adding a brand. When market researchers recognize a new consumer trend, senior executives charged with portfolio management must get involved to avoid a familiar outcome: a number of similar products for similar customers and need states.

Those executives also should take a clean-sheet approach to the company's collection of brands every three to five years. The purpose is to reassess each element of the company's portfolio perspective, including the frame of reference (particularly the markets in which each brand competes), the roles of current brands, and the need for fewer (or more) brands. External events, such as acquisitions or substantial innovations, also may necessitate a full-fledged portfolio review.

Using a thoughtful portfolio approach to restrain the temptation to brand can pay big dividends. For companies that succeed, portfolio management becomes not a onetime event, but a living, breathing part of day-to-day business.

The authors wish to thank Jonathan Gordon, Tamara Jurgenson, Thomas Meyer, and Jürgen Schröder for their contributions to this chapter.

•

Steve Carlotti (steve_carlotti@mckinsey.com), **Mary Ellen Coe** (mary_ellen_coe@mckinsey.com), and **Jesko Perrey** (jesko_perrey@mckinsey.com) are members of McKinsey's global marketing sales practice.
Steve Carlotti is a director and Mary Ellen Coe is a principal in McKinsey's Chicago office; and Jesko Perrey is a principal in the Düsseldorf office.

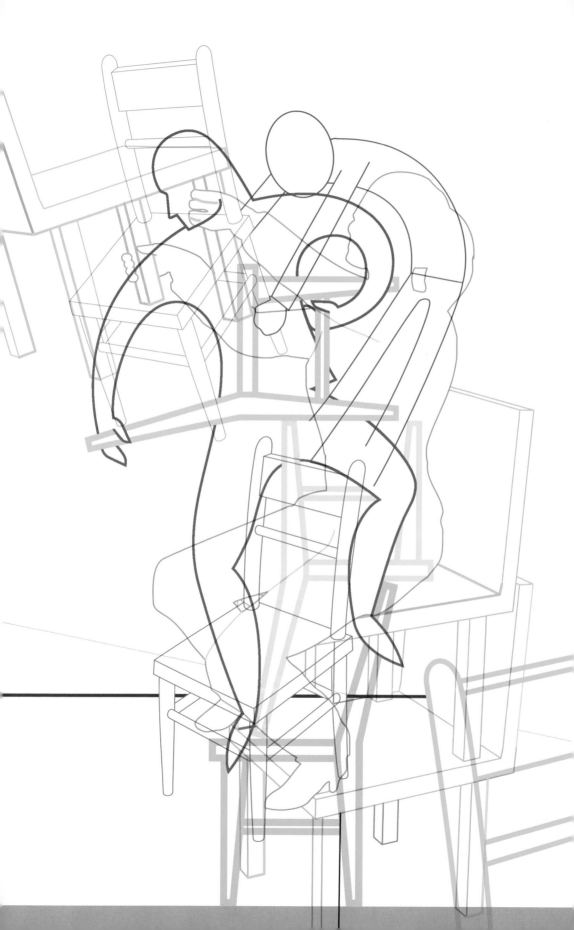

Finding growth opportunities with a customer insights network

John E. Forsyth, Nicolo' Galante,
and Todd Guild

In a marketing environment dominated by proliferation, stimulating growth requires a deep understanding of customer needs and behavior at the intersection of segments, channels, and product categories. By focusing on these intersection points, marketers can avoid averaging out customer preferences that, if properly understood, might suggest new opportunities (see sidebar, "Six trends that matter for marketers" on page 40). Companies can find advantages in the crazy quilt of proliferating segments, brands, channels, and communication vehicles if they identify and prioritize clusters of the highest-value, fastest-growing *customer cells* (groupings of customers whose common characteristics are best identified when viewed from multiple angles) and then develop cell-level marketing and sales programming.

Most companies, though, still regard customer insights as an isolated research capability. As a result, they can neither obtain data at the points where segments, channels, and categories intersect nor integrate the information to generate valuable insights. The isolation of the insights capability also inhibits the transformation of insights into actions and leaves many a company without a common way of looking at and describing customers. Instead, marketing focuses on brands; sales looks at geography, channel types, and key accounts; and market research views the world in segments.

The solution isn't to redraw boxes and lines on the organizational chart but rather to enhance the connections among the various actors needed to generate and act on cell-level insights. Of course, there's a term for a system of interconnecting parts that work together: a network. What companies need today is an *insights network* that helps them to look at the world through a number of lenses and to develop truly proprietary knowledge about customers. The network should not only integrate data on attitudes, behavior, transactions, and so forth but also encompass relationships with expert third parties (who can help companies manage complex data sets or master innovative qualitative-research techniques) and with key suppliers or customers (who can provide, for example, transactional data contributing to regional or store-level competitive intelligence).

Consider a consumer electronics company that struggled to increase its sales in the mass-market discount stores (such as Wal-Mart Stores), which were taking share from its traditional channels. Customary market research approaches couldn't isolate the cause of the problem. By integrating point-of-sale data with an online survey on shopping behavior in stores and general customer interests, the company learned that a surprisingly large number of people shopping for TVs at Wal-Mart were primarily interested in watching sports. This insight—combined with discrete-choice research on the TV features that sports-minded TV buyers valued most (picture-in-picture capabilities, digital connections, and plenty of audiovisual ports)—highlighted an opportunity to change the mix and features of products the company sold at Wal-Mart and to focus in-store marketing on sports fans.

To capitalize on such insights, companies must embed them in the organization's key decisions by restructuring brand and sales planning, new-product development, marketing investments, and other business-planning processes. By working across geographies and functions to gather common sets of information from the field and to translate the resulting insights into frontline actions—in other words, by behaving in an integrated, networked way—brand, sales, and key-account managers can improve a whole company's ability to make decisions.

Capturing growth at intersection points

Companies can now glean increasingly impressive and potentially lucrative insights by, for example, sharpening their focus on the customer at the point of purchase. A few insights-driven companies have taken this lesson to heart and begun pursuing cell-level customer intelligence and applying it to their marketing and sales endeavors. Consider the following examples.

- One aspect of the European grocer Tesco's approach to understanding customers is focusing on opportunities at the intersection of needs-based customer segments and product category sales in the company's four main store formats (Express, Metro, Extra, and supermarkets).[1] For example, by combining loyalty card data on what customers were buying at Tesco with survey research on what customers were not buying, Tesco found that, in some formats, young mothers bought fewer baby products in its stores because they trusted pharmacies more. So Tesco launched BabyClub to provide expert advice and targeted coupons. Its share of baby product sales in the United Kingdom grew from 16 percent in 2000 to 24 percent in 2003.

- Best Buy is renewing its store formats by integrating shopper research, point-of-sale data, and demographic analysis to determine which shopper segments are over- and underrepresented in certain areas and then varying its store formats accordingly. Stores located near large concentrations of affluent male professionals, for example, offer more high-end home theater equipment, specialized financing, and same-day delivery. Stores closer to soccer moms feature softer colors, personal-shopping assistants, and kid-oriented technology sections. After these stores changed to the target formats, tests showed that sales surged by 7 percent and the gross profit rate jumped by 50 basis points.

- Recently, a fixed-line telecom provider integrated a telephone survey of its customers' shopping behavior, Internet use, and telecom needs with the contents of its internal data warehouse, which links demographics to consumption profiles across local, long-distance, data, and broadband services. This analysis revealed an insufficient marketing focus on affluent households with heavy Internet use, so the company reoriented its mix of advertising vehicles (toward more Web-based advertising) and channel promotions (toward store chains visited by Web-savvy customers).

Notwithstanding these success stories, few companies have defined an approach or developed the necessary skills for synthesizing insights across

---

[1] Needs-based segments consist of groups of customers at the intersection of what people want and how they want to buy it. For more on need-state segmentation, see "Designing and managing winning brand portfolios," on page 20.

brands, channels, products, and regions. One reason is that brand teams, market research groups, regional sales teams, and channel partners have different views of the world (Exhibit 1). As a result, each group looks for and generates different, often unrelated, customer data from the overwhelming volume available. One consumer products company has marketers who segment end consumers in elaborate ways but a distribution organization that develops channel strategies based simply on retailer types. These differences make it difficult to integrate channel-, segment-, and brand-level data—and virtually impossible to collaborate on understanding and targeting high-value customer cells.

Even when companies generate sets of insights that could inform the sales and marketing actions they take at the cell level, organizational disconnects often make it hard to translate those insights into coordinated activities. A beer company, for example, knows that the battle for growth against brands of wine and spirits takes place in defined locations in specific geographies. It has also determined which consumer segments to target in which type of bar and restaurant chain. But until recently, its marketers still gave the sales force and its distribution partners brand plans that described broad national marketing programs rather than helping sales and distribution teams to understand how they might use more detailed, local key-account or channel insights. As a result, the company failed to exploit its cell-level insights.

EXHIBIT 1

Disconnected views

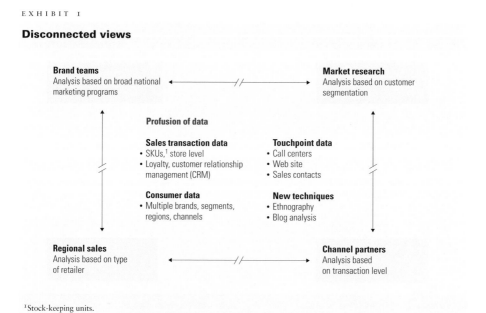

[1] Stock-keeping units.

Creating an insights network

Companies can integrate data, generate insights, and convert them into cell-level activities by starting with information from diverse sources and then instituting a shared, cross-functional approach and a common set of skills within an insights network of practitioners. This network often includes customer and third-party partners who help provide and analyze data.

Managing insights data

The first step in establishing an insights network is defining what sources of data the company needs. These sources typically include a subset of "foundational" data (such as market- and channel-level sales or category data) that a company's functional units develop in common and share. Then the company should integrate its basic data with more nuanced information on customers or shoppers or with data from loyalty club cards, points of sale and scanners, quantitative surveys, qualitative interviews, and other sources of knowledge to which it has privileged, if not fully proprietary, access.

Since the goal is to look at customers through a variety of lenses, the company should ask itself whether the sources selected will, collectively, tell it who its current (or potential) customers are; what they want; when, where, and why they buy; and how much they are worth. For a telecom company, basic data sources might include individual subscribers' usage profiles and demographic information, along with market research on the communications needs of different household segments. For a retailer, basic data sources might include loyalty card and point-of-sale data, which could be combined with region-specific shopper-segmentation data and with in- and out-of-store market research on the drivers of shoppers' behavior. As a company pursues new sources of growth, its frame of reference will likely expand from current to prospective customers. Its research focus must change accordingly.

Many companies find it important to add qualitative observations of customers; P&G's practice of observing them in their daily routines is one well-known example. Among retailers and apparel makers, a common tool today is the closet check: going into homes and looking in the closets and drawers to see what people wear.

For most companies, the key to extracting powerful cell-level insights from all this information is the very human task of analyzing the different data sources and then relating them, through active problem solving, to key business decisions. It's critical to involve a diverse array of people, including some with regional knowledge, others with trade or pricing skills, and still others with skills in branding or key-account management.

An example of how all this works in practice comes from the experience of a European battery supplier that tried to boost its sales at a powerful retailer. The supplier noticed that its highest-margin, "high-tech" batteries were frequently out of stock there. Believing that high-tech users were driving demand, it responded with a prominent new display rack describing the more expensive battery's benefits for digital devices. But instead of rising as expected, sales actually fell.

Only after the company conducted a series of studies at a local hypermarket did it understand this counterintuitive customer response. Exit interviews with people who purchased batteries clarified why they did so, and in-store observation showed how they shopped. In fact, few of these people were buying the more expensive high-tech product for digital devices; instead, they bought it in the belief that it lasted longer (a fact not emphasized in the displays) or by simple chance. The company returned to the original display in the do-it-yourself section and created a new high-tech-only display for the multimedia one. Sales in pilot stores then shot up by 20 percent because customers no longer had the impression that the main reason to buy the batteries was their performance in digital devices. This well-targeted response resulted from the company's effectiveness at integrating point-of-

Six trends that matter for marketers

Better insights can help marketers recognize and take advantage of important consumer trends. Six of them are described here. While many aren't new, they now have an increasingly profound impact on marketing.

1. *Age dynamics.* Young consumers in many developing countries are spending more money, watching more TV, listening to more radio, and talking more on their (cell) phones than ever before. Meanwhile, baby boomers in developed countries are getting older, living longer, and still buying a wide range of products because many remain young at heart. The challenge for global marketers is to develop growth strategies for both ends of the age spectrum while creating brand positionings that won't turn off aging baby boomers who don't want to feel old.

2. *Process and relationship benefits.* In industries from cars and cosmetics to credit cards and telecommunications, functional product benefits are taking a backseat to process benefits (which make

commercial transactions easier, quicker, cheaper, and more pleasant) and relationship benefits (which reward the willingness of consumers to identify themselves and reveal their purchasing behavior). One reason for the change is the way time pressures and stress are continuing to put a premium on convenience, simplicity, and speed. Marketers should therefore focus more intently on processes and relationships. One company that has done so is Amazon.com, with its one-click ordering and personalized product recommendations.

3. *Complex consumption "occasions."* Consumers increasingly demand variety in where, when, and how they consume products and services. So companies must create—and marketers must promote—a broader set of product packaging and service formats. Coca-Cola has taken this road by increasing its range of bottle and can sizes. Fast-food providers such as Pizza Hut and Taco Bell have augmented their traditional restaurants with airport, express, and gas station formats.

sale data and general category knowledge with findings from surveys and observations in the channel.

Collaborating with insights partners

In addition to involving each of the key marketing and sales functions, more insight-driven companies are enlisting a new set of partners and third-party research providers, which can boost the odds of developing cell-level insights.

Channel partners. Manufacturers, upstream suppliers, and downstream retailers should learn to collaborate on the basis of shared insights, since their data sets are complementary. Retailers often have transactional data describing what takes place in a product category at a very discrete level. At the other end of the channel, branded manufacturers have rich information, by segment and region, about consumer relationships with their brands and categories.

Sharing such insights can yield powerful results for either or both parties. One of Alcoa's cardboard suppliers, for example, shared its research findings about the way consumers replace soda in their refrigerators. The aluminum manufacturer then pitched a new refrigerator-friendly package to Coca-Cola—a proposal that contributed to a 10 percent uptick in Coke's sales

---

4. *Discerning consumers in a polarizing world.* Products from beer, clothes, and computers to refrigerators are becoming polarized between high- and low-end offerings. Meanwhile, consumers, who are increasingly likely to purchase private-label goods in one category and premium goods in another, are placing extraordinary emphasis on value across the whole product and service spectrum. These tendencies help account for the success of retailers such as Tesco, with their price architectures differentiating among "good," "better," and "best" products, and for the declining effectiveness of merchandise strategies that emphasize periodic price promotions. The challenge for marketers is to integrate focused offerings and tailored promotions that will attract today's "no-nonsense" consumers at both ends of the market.

5. *Product and service referrals.* Distrust of big business, big government, and advertising is rampant: more than half of the respondents to a 2005 Yankelovich Partners survey, for example, said that they resisted paying attention to advertisements. But consumers are increasingly receptive to referrals by friends or trusted experts. Marketing strategies that emphasize the generation of brand references will grow in importance.

6. *Global brands.* Tastes are globalizing, as shown, for example, by the growing diversity of the Asian foods available in Western supermarkets. Consumers who have more experience with foreign brands are embracing them more enthusiastically, from Western Europeans who buy Haier refrigerators to people in China who buy high-tech goods from South Korea. But the purveyors of large global brands shouldn't be complacent. Our research shows only a limited correlation between the age of brands and their strength. Indeed, in many emerging markets, such as China and India, national brands are challenging global ones—and striving for global reach themselves.

during the three months after the package was introduced. Another example comes from Wal-Mart, generally considered to be the only retailer in Europe that can collect and organize clean and consistent electronic point-of-sale data. Through Wal-Mart's Retail Link tool, the company provides this information to key suppliers online, thus helping not only them but also itself because, in return, the suppliers share the results of some of their own analyses.

Vendor partners. The network must also include vendor partners that specialize in developing insights and will likely require a company to shift its business from relationship-driven, full-service vendors to firms with unique abilities to probe the intersection of different types of information. Such vendors include data-cleansing houses and predictive-modeling shops, anthropologist networks, in-context interview specialists, and firms that mine retailers' transaction records. The expertise that such vendors provide is difficult (and expensive) for marketers to build within their own companies.

The marketers' exchanges with vendors will shift from outsourcing low-value tasks and commissioning tactical research (such as concept tests) to identifying cell-level opportunities. So the process of working with vendors must also shift, from an assembly line for processing data—the marketer poses hypotheses, the vendor conducts research, and the analyst interprets the data—to a collaborative effort involving joint data collection and analysis. Collaboration yields a larger number of connections between marketers and vendor partners and a more sustained set of relationships, which together help marketing and sales organizations build the skills they need to develop cell-level insights.

Embedding insights in key decisions

To be valuable, cell-level insights must help companies to develop integrated marketing and sales activities spanning their product-development, brand, sales, category-management, and key-account teams. Making this happen requires a shift from managing insights primarily within a single function, as most companies have traditionally done, to embedding them in the planning processes and resource allocation decisions that guide all marketing activities.

Insight-driven decision processes

To embed insights in the way companies make their most important marketing and sales decisions, they must address the underlying processes that shape those decisions. Consider the following examples.

Marketing planning. Traditionally, insights about customers have informed certain elements of marketing or brand planning—for instance, setting priorities for raising (or defending) market share across a portfolio of brands, targeting high-potential customer segments or channels, and allocating advertising and promotional investments. One packaged-goods company has combined such familiar marketing-plan practices with new, cell-level insights, such as shopping habits in a key channel's core consumer segment. These insights in turn influence the company's channel-level packaging and pricing plans. Embedding insights more deeply in marketing plans calls for well-connected analysts and marketing managers. They must have incentives not only to integrate channel-based insights about shoppers with traditional insights about the way core segments see brands but also to work with brand, product and packaging, and field sales teams to use this analysis in refining plans and decisions.

Product development. Companies can use insights to identify new-product opportunities and make more intelligent decisions about whether to continue financing ideas at different stages of development. A cell phone manufacturer looking for promising offerings in several profitable markets, for example, established customer segment panels, whose members were asked to maintain diaries detailing where and how they used PDAs and wireless devices. With this information in hand, the company's brand and segment managers could ensure, at key stage-gate points in product development, that the teams of developers were truly meeting the needs of target customer segments in critical markets by proposing appropriate new-product and packaged-service ideas, such as business- or entertainment-oriented browser interface designs. These managers also helped to create the sales plans needed to focus the new offers on targeted customer cells. It's difficult to see how the usual practices, such as developing ideas for new products based on leading technology or market trends, could yield similar results.

Account planning. Companies can significantly improve their key-account plans by combining data from retailers with insights from suppliers. The resulting rich trove of information could be used to develop not only account-specific, regional, and even store-level product ranges, mixes, and pricing targets (including in-store promotional programming and priorities) but also category-management goals for large accounts.

The importance of cross-functional integration
Insights can inform key decisions only when people in a company—especially its marketing and sales professionals—work well across functions. Facilitating cross-functionality often requires clarifying who in the organization will play key insight-related roles. These responsibilities include incorporating channel-, region-, and customer-specific insights into plans for brands, products, packaging, and pricing, as well as generating key-account plans that help

salespeople take advantage of insights about shoppers and of intelligence developed through collaboration with channel partners.

The key challenge typically isn't resources; the people already work somewhere in the organization. Rather, it's ensuring that they have access to common sets of data, use a common set of approaches, have the right skills, and work in a coordinated way. Here's how a tire manufacturer achieved these goals:

- The company identified people from sales, marketing, and market research who would combine their cell insights to develop an integrated view of channel opportunities. Members of the sales organization collected volume data from retailers; people in the marketing department conducted research into shopping behavior; and colleagues in the market research group surveyed shoppers in different channels and undertook a conjoint analysis of the results.

- By integrating these insights, the cross-functional group identified product lines the company could charge a premium for without encouraging consumers to switch to discount channels.

- Finally, the group worked through established brand-, sales-, and business-planning processes to develop account plans that articulated, for each customer, the insight-driven rationale of changes in pricing policy.

As this example shows, the brand, sales, and channel managers who play key insight-related roles don't have to be new hires or devote all of their time to the effort. Rather, the company reallocated them for a period from their original functions and managed them through a common approach based on the use of shared data and analytical tools.

Suppose a business that manages insights as a functional responsibility wants to switch to developing a company-wide capability that could benefit from the involvement of far-flung participants (Exhibit 2). First, there must be a top-down commitment—usually driven by the CEO, the CMO, and the head of sales—to work in accord with common practices and definitions concerning insights. The CMO and the head of sales should play a governance role by resolving conflicts about brand, channel, and regional priorities and by setting growth goals at the cell level. They must also promote the use of a common language for insights and of shared metrics for the performance of brands or categories and for channels, segments, and

EXHIBIT 2

Characteristics of an insights-driven company

Building a company-wide capability	• Leaders' vision, support, and alignment • Distinctive customer insights capabilities
Embedding insights into frontline decisions	• Consistent insight-driven execution • Integrated, iterative planning and commercial processes
Generating proprietary insights at the cell[1] level	• Network of strategic partners • Proprietary data sets, innovative tools • Focus on fast-growing, high-value customer cells[1]

[1] Groupings of customers whose common characteristics are best identified by viewing the intersection of segments, channels, product categories, store formats, or communication vehicles.

regions. While the idea of such metrics may seem straightforward, adopting them takes many companies at least two annual planning cycles. Finally, senior executives shouldn't overlook the role of social skills and of what Daniel Goleman calls "emotional intelligence" in making collaborative processes work.[2] By hiring and developing people with these skills and qualities, companies can improve the performance of an insights network.

———————

Today's proliferating marketing environment creates opportunities to outsmart and outgrow competitors by generating and acting on cell-level customer insights. To do so, marketing and sales organizations must first create an insights network that mobilizes partners to generate and analyze the appropriate data and then embed the relevant capabilities in the organization's key planning and decision-making processes.

[2] Daniel Goleman, *Emotional Intelligence: Why It Can Matter More than IQ*, reprint edition, New York, NY: Bantam, 1997.

The authors would like to thank Yoram Gutgeld and David Sackin for their contributions to this chapter.

•

John Forsyth (john_forsyth@mckinsey.com), **Nicolo' Galante** (nicolo_galante@mckinsey.com), and **Todd Guild** (todd_guild@mckinsey.com) are members of McKinsey's global marketing and sales practice. John Forsyth is a principal in McKinsey's Stamford office, Nicolo' Galante is a principal in the Milan office, and Todd Guild is a director in the Tokyo office.

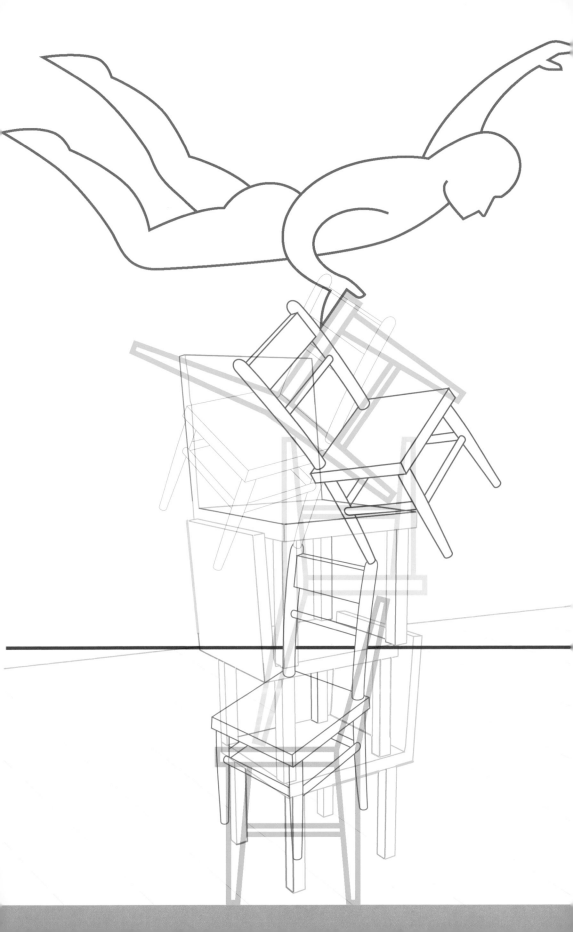

Transforming sales and service

**Thomas Baumgartner, Roland H. John,
and Tomas Nauclér**

As sales and service channels proliferate, customers in a wide range of industries are finding it easier to mix and match suppliers in order to achieve the holy grail of simple, low-cost support for some needs and deep knowledge and collaboration for others.[1] This phenomenon is particularly problematic for business-to-business (B2B) suppliers, whose traditional competitive advantages, based on superior products and relationships, are under pressure for well-known reasons: purchasing organizations are getting more sophisticated, low-cost competitors from China and India are becoming increasingly prevalent, and innovations are being imitated more rapidly.[2]

With no place left to hide, B2B suppliers must turn to their go-to-market model—including sales, sales support, and service—which is a powerful factor in the purchasing decisions of many customers (Exhibit 1, on the next page). Unfortunately, developing a winning go-to-market model isn't easy for incumbent suppliers. Their basic transaction costs are too high for

---

[1] For more on collaborative selling, see Maryanne Q. Hancock, Roland H. John, and Philip J. Wojcik, "Better B2B selling," *The McKinsey Quarterly*, Web exclusive, June 2005 (www.mckinseyquarterly.com/links/21039).
[2] For more on these challenges, see John M. Abele, William K. Caesar, and Roland H. John, "Rechanneling sales," *The McKinsey Quarterly*, 2003 Number 3, pp. 64–75 (www.mckinseyquarterly.com/links/21040).

them to compete with no-frills specialists—for instance, Chi Mei in chemicals and High Tech Computer (HTC) in technology. And they don't have enough expertise in industry-specific solutions to compete with businesses (such as GE Plastics and IBM Global Services) that are setting new standards for value-added sales and service.

This "stuck-in-the-middle" scenario is playing out across a wide range of industries, including advanced materials, chemicals, information technology, and telecommunications. It can leave companies vulnerable to attack from both sides. More than one global supplier has recently lost a substantial share of its revenue both to Asian attackers with far lower costs and to genuine solutions specialists offering faster, more sophisticated service.

If incumbents had the luxury of choosing to sell in just one end of the market, the answer to these difficulties might be simple. But focusing in this way means giving up economies of scale and scope, and there aren't enough high-end customers to support a mass retreat to the stratosphere. Suppliers must instead continue serving the whole market. But how? Not by adding Band-Aid-like technical sales teams with limited competence in delivering

EXHIBIT I

The quality of interaction counts

Enterprise telecom products/services,[1] % of contribution to purchase decision

Factors affecting decision to purchase

Sales	10	
Building, installation	13	Customer interaction = 44%
Operations, maintenance, repair	21	
Product features/ type of offering	27	
Price, cost savings	27	
Company's image	—2	

Customer interaction process

Sales	Building, installation	Operations
• Identifiable contact person	• Adherence to project plan	• Identifiable contact person
• Speed of issuing offer	• Transparency of project plan	• Speed of repairs
• Competence in negotiating	• Translation of customer needs into project plan	• Competence of help desk
• Speed of response		• Accuracy of invoice
• Professionalism, fairness in negotiations	• Quality of project management	• Clarity of invoice
• Quality of information		
• Transparency of order status		

[1] Corporate networks, desktop services, integrated voice-data networks, Internet access, landline voice services.

Source: Customer interviews and focus groups; McKinsey analysis

solutions or by creating new transactional channels, which often create cost and complexity problems and sometimes even reduce customer satisfaction. Rather, they need a clean-sheet redesign based on what customers want from their sales and service interactions and what kind of organizational structure is necessary to provide that kind of support efficiently and effectively.

Rethinking the approach

More specifically, to cut costs and enhance the customer experience, companies should take three steps:

1. Identify the company's full range of sales and service situations, from simple transactions to complex consulting arrangements.

2. Build a high-quality, low-cost platform of sales support and service processes for interactions that cut across all customers. This *lean backbone* typically encompasses efforts to supply customers with information as well as order entry, fulfillment, training, and after-sales service.

3. Develop affordable standard modules (or high-touch overlays) for situations where customers value additional sales or service support enough to cover its cost. These modules might include teams of industry experts, application-development teams, and "hunting" teams focused on acquiring new customers.

Ambitious as this approach may seem, it's already happening. For example, as Dell's corporate and government business has grown to represent roughly three-fourths of the company's sales, Dell has retained a lean backbone based on Internet and telesales transactions and service while providing value-added services for major buyers.

More recently, a few large sales- and service-oriented companies in Asia, Europe, and North America have moved out from the middle by redesigning their go-to-market approaches. One advanced-materials manufacturer that was losing market share to low-end specialists and not capturing the full growth potential of the high-end customer segment identified four core sales and service situations. To support all four of them, the company built a backbone that includes order handling, billing, invoicing, and logistics management. Finally, it developed standardized overlays (such as consultative sales, joint R&D, and application-development teams) that it combines in various ways to provide distinctive support in each sales and service interaction (Exhibit 2). Together, these efforts helped the company to cut its selling, general, and administrative (SG&A) costs by 20 percent and to triple the growth rate of its new products.

Focusing on sales and service needs

The go-to-market organizations of B2B suppliers rarely create profiles of different sales and service interactions, analyze how frequently they take place, or understand what makes the difference between competitive success and failure in each. Many companies therefore devote too many sales and service resources to simple transactions and too few to complex ones where the key differentiator might be the deep domain expertise of, say, a technical sales team that really knows how cutting-edge products

EXHIBIT 2

Best of both worlds

Disguised example of advanced-materials company

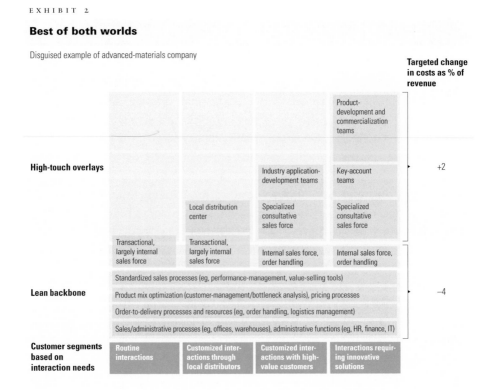

Targeted change in costs as % of revenue

			Product-development and commercialization teams	
High-touch overlays			Industry application-development teams	Key-account teams	+2
		Local distribution center	Specialized consultative sales force	Specialized consultative sales force	
	Transactional, largely internal sales force	Transactional, largely internal sales force	Internal sales force, order handling	Internal sales force, order handling	
Lean backbone	Standardized sales processes (eg, performance-management, value-selling tools)				−4
	Product mix optimization (customer-management/bottleneck analysis), pricing processes				
	Order-to-delivery processes and resources (eg, order handling, logistics management)				
	Sales/administrative processes (eg, offices, warehouses), administrative functions (eg, HR, finance, IT)				
Customer segments based on interaction needs	Routine interactions	Customized interactions through local distributors	Customized interactions with high-value customers	Interactions requiring innovative solutions	

work. Companies should thus begin rethinking their approach by deciding exactly what type and quality of sales and service interaction they must provide to their various customers.

To grasp the difference that focusing on sales and service interactions can make, consider the case of a global network components provider that until recently was stuck in the middle between low-cost competitors from Asia and companies that won high-end customers by offering new solutions and stronger field expertise. This company had failed to differentiate among the various types of interactions buyers needed, instead assigning to each of them an account manager plus technical sales and service personnel.

Analysis revealed that 70 percent of this company's customer interactions, across buyers of all sizes, were relatively simple—involving the provision and untailored installation and configuration of standard products such as routers and switches. An additional 10 percent of its interactions involved mature but complex networks requiring some customization. Only 20 percent of the time did a nascent technology call for the development of truly new solutions, such as next-generation all-Internet-protocol networks (Exhibit 3, on the next page).

Matching the needs and service levels of customers more effectively helped the company reduce its overall go-to-market costs by nearly 20 percent. By concentrating its expertise on those interactions that truly require special know-how, it also improved the quality of its customization work and speeded up the development of new solutions. The company now manages their development centrally and transforms them as quickly as possible into standard packages suitable for large numbers of customers. It does so, in part, by consolidating ideas for new solutions that arise in different geographies and by centrally coordinating their design and development.

Boosting service quality and reducing costs with a lean backbone

Whenever a company profiles its sales and service interactions, it will recognize possibilities for standardization. These typically include transactional interactions (such as order entry, processing, and tracking), the provision of product information, and simple customer service (including basic training and after-sales support). Companies should strive to carry out these interactions in a way that is highly cost effective and consistent, so that customers making any type of purchase have the same experience executing transactions, obtaining information, and receiving basic service.

EXHIBIT 3

Toward a better match

Disguised example of global network components company

From segmentation based on customer size . . .

- Does not differentiate sales or delivery for different offerings, customers
- Offers no cost competitiveness on standard offerings and does not encourage uptake of new products, offerings

. . . to segmentation based on customer's interaction requirements and complexity of offering

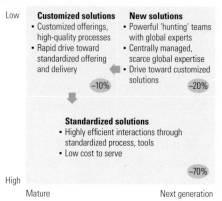

- Improves sales, profitability by reallocating scarce technical resources to new-solutions segment
- Increases profitability by significantly reducing cost to serve for standardized solutions

xx% Typical % of customers within segment

This approach typically involves centralizing many of these activities and then adopting a lean philosophy that emphasizes the elimination of waste and rework, the standardization of processes, and continuous improvement. The resulting sales and service delivery system contrasts markedly with the norm at many companies: operating in a more ad hoc way, with each business, segment, and channel often having its own sales and service infrastructure.

To understand the power of a lean backbone, consider the experience of a major telecommunications operator that couldn't satisfy its customers' desire for an accurate, efficient transaction system. Customers' expectations had been raised by promises of one-stop service from multidisciplinary teams that were to handle everything from ordering and changing service to billing issues, service interruptions, and customer complaints. But the complex structure of the multidisciplinary teams undermined their effectiveness, particularly compared with the service offered by focused competitors that provided only data, network, or voice support. The teams were also extremely expensive and became more so as they sought to compensate for breakdowns by providing higher and higher levels of service.

The solution was to create a lean backbone that met the customers' interaction needs more cost effectively. For starters, the company separated all of its routine and offline customer care efforts from its live, high-touch interactions. Next, it standardized work processes and the way it captured information, thus allowing itself to organize the offline efforts into more efficient regional and national "transaction factories" that created economies of scale and improved the company's execution. It then encouraged customers to migrate their routine work and inquiries to electronic channels, reserving live interactions for the resolution of complex problems. (The multidisciplinary teams, relieved of transactional responsibilities, became a high-touch overlay for select customer interactions.) These changes not only cut the company's customer care costs by 25 percent, through the consolidation of 14 customer care centers into 7, but also improved response times and boosted satisfaction.

It's not unusual for a consistent, heavily automated lean backbone to boost the quality of a company's customer interactions and to reduce their costs by executing transactions quickly and flawlessly the first time around. A utility that standardized its call-center and customer service processes and its online channels raised its customer satisfaction scores to 85 percent, from 70, while costs in the affected areas fell by 40 percent.

Adding affordable high-touch overlays

In some situations, competitive differentiation demands truly distinctive sales or service. A key-account team that includes product-development experts might be needed to close deals involving new products. Or a rapid-response technical-service team could be essential for customers using the supplier's products in mission-critical applications.

A lot of these high-touch situations share enough elements that companies can address them in a standardized fashion. Unfortunately, many companies do anything but. They allocate sales and service resources in an imprecise, decentralized way, with each business, segment, or channel manager establishing the teams he or she needs. These companies squander scale economies, duplicate efforts, and leave the door open for frontline managers to create inefficient customer service models. The better approach is to establish standard overlay configurations that define what is and isn't included in key-account, application-development, or technical-service teams. Local decision makers should then select the best overlay for their particular situation.

The development of affordable, consistent overlays calls for a disciplined, investment-oriented approach with clear cost guidelines and strict approval rules. For sales overlays, the big challenge is determining whether a higher-touch effort—say, the use of a key-account team—will justify its cost by increasing the likelihood of closing deals, engendering loyalty, or winning preferential treatment. In after-sales service, the questions are whether customers will pay for the higher service level the overlay provides and how to ensure that the right customers are using it. For instance, at the network components provider described previously, the global sales and marketing manager must approve the costly deployment of solutions-development teams.

One IT hardware and software producer used overlays to streamline a sales approach that involved serving six segments through ten distinct channels, including four types of sales teams and two types of external partners as well as retail, online, and telesales channels. The resulting complexity made it difficult for the company to focus its salespeople on the right opportunities, quickly complete simple processes (such as supplying price quotes or responding to customer bids), and provide competitive high-end solutions. In addition, the company operated at a significant cost disadvantage relative to most of its competitors.

Gaining control over its channels meant building a lean backbone comprising uniform Web and telesales operations and then augmenting it with overlays that met rigorous affordability guidelines. Developing these guidelines is a highly industry- and company-specific process that typically involves best-practice benchmarking and a careful analysis of sales team costs (Exhibit 4). Effective guidelines help differentiate between the overlays received by customers with the most sophisticated needs and those for high-volume customers. Clear guidelines also show what overlays should be received by customer segments within each of these broad groups. The technology company, for example, provided its most demanding customers with support from permanent teams led by senior account managers. To serve the next tier of high-value customers, the company assigned sales representatives who could quickly mobilize presale support and product or service specialists. High-volume customers, on the other hand, relied heavily on the lean backbone (often supplemented by a

EXHIBIT 4

What can we afford?

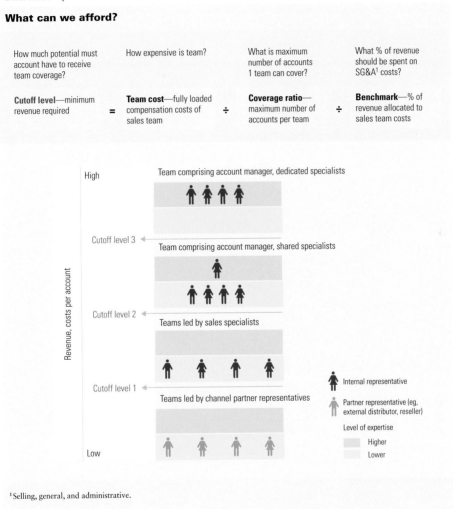

How much potential must account have to receive team coverage?	How expensive is team?	What is maximum number of accounts 1 team can cover?	What % of revenue should be spent on SG&A[1] costs?
Cutoff level—minimum revenue required $=$	**Team cost**—fully loaded compensation costs of sales team $\div$	**Coverage ratio**— maximum number of accounts per team $\div$	**Benchmark**—% of revenue allocated to sales team costs

High

Team comprising account manager, dedicated specialists

Cutoff level 3

Team comprising account manager, shared specialists

Cutoff level 2

Teams led by sales specialists

Cutoff level 1

Teams led by channel partner representatives

Low

Revenue, costs per account

Internal representative

Partner representative (eg, external distributor, reseller)

Level of expertise

Higher

Lower

[1] Selling, general, and administrative.

personalized purchasing Web site). But some received additional support from channel partners, others were assigned remote sales and support specialists, and the most valuable got face-to-face support that helped iron out presale details.

These changes created a sales support system that was better and cheaper than the one it replaced, but they also made it necessary to reassign a substantial number of accounts to new sales and service personnel and to eliminate direct coverage for certain customers. To fend off competitors trying to exploit this flux, the company accepted some short-term channel redundancy (among other things) to ease the transition and mounted campaigns to make customers aware of how the new approaches—for instance, a dedicated Web site for volume purchases—would meet their needs more fully than the cumbersome account teams had. (For more on channel migration, see sidebar, "Managing the transition.")

Putting the pieces together

Transforming a corporate go-to-market organization by resegmenting customers, redesigning the sales and service backbone, and introducing standardized overlays amount to a major undertaking that often takes from 18 to 36 months. In our experience, the keys to success include sequencing initiatives carefully to generate cost and revenue benefits in the early months, building skills in a focused manner, and enforcing new forms of account-

Managing the transition

No matter how good a company's new go-to-market strategy may be, the business can founder if customers think that service is deteriorating or if problems with channel partners and employees emerge. The secret to managing the transition is getting the timing right, providing safety nets that help customers deal with change, and using incentives to guide customers and assuage channel partners.[1]

Getting the timing right

It is easier to open up new channels if supplies are tight, demand is strong, or competitors are in decline, because these conditions reduce the likelihood that customers or channel partners will defect. When a particular class of chemicals was in short supply, for example, one leading manufacturer migrated its transactionally oriented customers, representing more than 20 percent of its accounts and 10 percent of its volume, to telesales. That move freed up face-to-face salespeople to focus on new prospects that were promising but time consuming to develop, as product demonstrations were required. To make the migration easier, the company placed experienced salespeople in the telesales role—a tactic that helped customers to accept the lack of face-to-face contact and to preserve preexisting relationships—even when supplies were no longer short.

Providing safety nets

Customers often require access to the touchpoints of both the old and the new channels, as well as hands-on training in the new one. W. W. Grainger, a large US supplier of maintenance, repair, and operations (MRO) parts, provided for these needs when it migrated customers from its personal sales staff to the Internet without making them less satisfied with its service. The company's 1,200-strong face-to-face sales force visited customers to show them how to order parts using the new Web-based system. Grainger made sure that its salespeople would invest enough energy in these training activities by adjusting its compensation system to give them credit for all sales in their territories, regardless of the channel. Today the sales reps spend much of their time on higher-value activities, such as finding new prospects and building customer loyalty, while the company has raised its e-commerce sales from less than $100 million in 1999 to nearly $500 million in 2003.

ability. The experience of the advanced-materials company mentioned earlier, which redesigned the work done by 10 percent of its employees in five business units and 50 countries, illustrates each of these points.

Sequencing

Establishing the lean backbone is typically the most challenging aspect of reorienting a company's sales and service model because the effort involves change throughout the organization. Nonetheless, such a backbone often provides the cost savings to finance the rest of the transformation, so companies should start creating it as soon as they identify their customers' shared sales and service needs.

In the case of the advanced-materials company, roughly a year was needed to consolidate invoicing, billing, and other support processes across Europe and to combine national sales offices by creating regional hubs.

Using incentives

Finally, it's important not to overlook the role of incentives. For customers, incentives frequently combine a "carrot" and a "stick." The carrot is something (typically, discounts or improved service) that customers value highly and receive only when they use the preferred channel. The stick might be fees or reduced service, both of which work best when they are reasonably opaque and switching costs are embedded in the product or service.

The thoughtful use of incentives also can help companies manage the response of their channel partners. A leading home-equipment manufacturer, for example, began selling products to big-box home-improvement centers despite the potential for conflict with its core channel, a dealer network. Before entering the home center channel, the manufacturer made sure that its dealers had strong financial incentives to continue pushing its products. First, it gave dealers a revenue stake in the new approach by ensuring that they handled postsales inspection and service on items purchased in home centers. Second, it gave dealers exclusive rights to certain product lines. In the end, the dealers significantly increased

their revenues from its products and services, since they captured incremental service revenues from a new customer segment and overall awareness of the brand increased. Meanwhile, the manufacturer made double-digit gains in market share.

Joseph B. Myers, Andrew D. Pickersgill, and Evan S. Van Metre

Joe Myers (joseph_myers@mckinsey.com), **Evan Van Metre** (evan_van_metre@mckinsey .com), and **Andrew Pickersgill** (andrew_ pickersgill@mckinsey.com) are members of McKinsey's global marketing and sales practice. Joe Myers and Evan Van Metre are principals in McKinsey's Atlanta office; Andrew Pickersgill is a principal in the Toronto office.

---

[1] For more on managing channel transitions, see Joseph B. Myers, Andrew D. Pickersgill, and Evan S. Van Metre, "Steering customers to the right channels," *The McKinsey Quarterly*, 2004 Number 4, pp. 36–47 (www.mckinseyquarterly.com/links/20903).

Within 18 months, the company had standardized its basic customer interactions, and its SG&A costs had fallen by 20 percent.

In year two, the company supplied its largest business unit with the overlays needed to create four new standard ways of interacting with customers. (One involved innovation-driven sales to global customers, another focused on value-added selling in national markets, and two were for customers with more standard needs.) The company first rolled out the overlays for the customers offering the greatest profit potential—for example, energy was the largest global segment and therefore an early target for innovation-oriented sales overlays. This approach made the rollout self-financing. Finally, in year three, the company implemented the new sales and service model in all of its business units.

Capability building

The standardization that is central to a cost-effective rollout of a new sales and service approach often requires that employees acquire new skills. The advanced-materials company had to dedicate nearly 5 percent of its sales force to helping all the other salespeople get comfortable with the lean backbone and the overlays—a process that took several years. One important element was learning how to use a new system to optimize the mix of orders that salespeople were seeking. To support the rollout, the company brought in 15 sales experts and built a sales academy. It also focused on *mini-transformations* (of, for example, the sales support associated with a particular overlay) in one national market and then applied what it had learned to its sales training in another one.

New forms of accountability

The advanced-materials company established clearer accountability for sales and service interactions by auditing, on a quarterly basis, its salespeople's efforts to use the lean backbone and the overlays. In addition, it created new operational targets (such as customer acquisition rates, time spent with customers, and customer service costs) for each of these interactions. The company therefore abandoned the practice of measuring performance by function; instead, all of the units involved with a specific type of interaction were held accountable for results.

Over three years, the company's careful focus on sequencing, building skills, and accountability helped cut its SG&A costs by 20 percent, triple its growth rate in the innovation-driven segments, and boost its return on capital employed by more than three percentage points.

———————————————————

Incumbents needn't remain stuck in the middle. To escape, they should rethink their customers' requirements, build a lean backbone to meet shared sales and service needs, and establish standard, high-touch overlays to satisfy more exacting demands cost effectively.

The authors wish to offer special thanks to Robert Hackl
and Johannes Pruchnow for their many contributions to the underlying ideas in this chapter.
They also wish to acknowledge the assistance of Peter Ewens, Jeff Schumacher,
Markus Weber, and more than 20 other colleagues.

•

Thomas Baumgartner (thomas_baumgartner@mckinsey.com), **Roland John**
(roland_john@mckinsey.com) and **Tomas Nauclér** (tomas_naucler@mckinsey.com) are members
of McKinsey's global marketing and sales practice. Thomas Baumgartner is
a director in McKinsey's Vienna office, Roland John is a director in the Atlanta office, and
Tomas Nauclér is a principal in the Stockholm office.

The power of a commercial operating system

Trond Riiber Knudsen, Cédric Moret, and Evan S. Van Metre

All too frequently, marketers' responses to proliferation undermine consistency, coordination, insight, and decision making. New brand, channel, and segment groups focus on increasingly disparate parts of the market and are often poorly integrated with the rest of the sales and marketing organization. Also, they give rise to unintended consequences, such as channel conflict, rising marketing costs, convoluted IT systems and other kinds of process infrastructure, and an inability to allocate marketing dollars consistently to the most valuable opportunities.

To understand these dynamics, consider the experience of a global beverage company dealing with three aspects of proliferation: the growth of the premium and economy segments at the expense of middle-of-the-road ones (the company's traditional focus), the increased importance of discount channels, and media proliferation. The company's responses—new brands, a variety of different segmentation strategies, and an increased emphasis on selling to discount retailers—added several layers of complexity to its marketing efforts.

As a result, the company's marketers had increasing difficulty identifying and pursuing opportunities in a coherent way, assigning accountability, and tracking performance. At the same time that brand managers in one region were investing in marketing communications to position a brand as a premium one, for example, the sales organization was discounting that brand for value-oriented retailers. These uncoordinated efforts eventually diluted the brand.

The solution to these problems was for the beverage maker to create what we call a *commercial operating system*—a blueprint for consistent sales and marketing in the two or three functional areas (such as pricing, brand, segment, channel, or key-account management) that are most closely linked to a company's strategic priorities. Most commercial operating systems have four well-integrated components (Exhibit 1):

- consistent processes, or sequences of activities along the business calendar, through which the relevant people interact to make high-quality marketing decisions

- leading-edge tools and frameworks to guide decision making

- clear responsibilities, skill requirements, and talent development for sales and marketing professionals in pivotal roles

EXHIBIT 1

A blueprint for consistency

Components of a commercial operating system

Framework and tools
Leading-edge methodologies, templates, tools, and ways of thinking that shape commercial decisions

Processes and interactions
Core marketing- and sales-management processes, including responsibilities, calendars, and interactions across organization

Talents and skills in pivotal roles
Right people and/or new skills developed in crucial positions that drive performance

Metrics and performance management
Set of standard metrics and explicit performance management across core processes

- consistent metrics and performance-management systems that reinforce the organization's processes, methodologies, and talent management

Although these elements might seem like standard attributes of any well-functioning marketing and sales organization, they are in fact far from common, as well as challenging to put in place and integrate. As a result, many companies have been disappointed by disjointed efforts to apply standard tools without clarifying who will make what decisions using the information the tools provide. Other companies redesign processes without linking them to measurable outcomes that matter to customers or improve skills without improving processes to take advantage of the new capabilities.

In this chapter we offer practical advice to marketers searching for more consistency, greater coordination, better insight, and improved decision making. We begin by laying out design principles that companies should follow when installing a commercial operating system. Then, to bring these principles to life, we describe several cases of companies that have upgraded the way they do marketing.

Designing a commercial operating system

The inconsistent, poorly coordinated marketing execution brought on by proliferation has severe consequences. Quality and efficiency suffer when companies let myriad disconnected brand, segment, and channel initiatives bloom. What's more, by increasing the number and role diversity of brand, segment, and channel managers, proliferation has complicated the interdependencies that have long existed within the marketing organization, making it not only less clear who is responsible for what but also virtually impossible to integrate different marketing and sales functions. And in recent years, as companies have been selling more products and brands to more segments in more channels and regions, while using more communications vehicles to advertise those products and brands, it has become more complex to measure and manage performance. To meet these challenges, companies must follow some important principles and avoid several pitfalls in the way they approach the integration of processes, tools, talent, and performance management.

Processes and interactions

Rather than upend the way everything is done, marketers should focus on the two or three key commercial processes that are central to superior business performance (Exhibit 2, on the next page). For a packaged-goods company,

EXHIBIT 2

Different strokes

Focus of commercial operating system

Process \ Company type	Profit, not volume — Industrial packaging	Service — Consumer packaging	Value marketing — Specialty chemicals	Customer life cycle — Financial services	Brand power — Logistics services
Consumer insights			●	●	●
Brand strategy		●			●
Product/service innovation			●		
Effectiveness of marketing spending				●	●
Channel/retailer management		●			
Business account management	●	●	●		
Sales force management	●			●	
Tactical promotion/ pricing	●				●

these processes might be advertising and innovation; for a paper manufacturer, they might be pricing and key-account management. Deciding where to focus requires attention to changes in the marketplace that sometimes demand new corporate priorities. If customers become more concentrated, for example, a company may need to develop key-account capabilities.

After selecting the processes, companies should avoid focusing exclusively on mechanics, such as the development of templates and checklists for employees to fill in and follow. Instead, executives should promote a healthy tension among decision makers in different parts of the organization. An important way of promoting the tension and dialogue that yield better decisions is to schedule periodic reviews during which top executives can challenge subordinates and each other about the relationships between seemingly uncoordinated marketing actions.

Frameworks and tools

Managing a portfolio of brands has long been more successful when all brand groups use a common approach to segmentation for their planning. Similarly, it's easier to set the right price when sales and marketing professionals conduct standard analyses to compare how much revenue a company keeps from each transaction. But proliferation has made consistency difficult to maintain, and advances in information technology have tempted many marketers to develop systems and tools so sophisticated that no one wants to use them.

To balance sophistication with consistency and user-friendliness, marketers should selectively determine which tools and frameworks to adopt or disseminate throughout the organization. Conceptual frameworks include sales funnels, which track the rate at which salespeople convert customers at each stage of the sales process, from prospecting and first meeting to proposal, sale, and contract. Tools might include information technology systems that automate and support the detailed analysis of the profitability of key accounts. Companies that select a small number of tools and frameworks capable of yielding a competitive advantage and then tailor them for widespread use are more likely to transform the increasingly complex information available into good decisions.

Talent and skills in pivotal roles

Frequently, a management role is inextricably linked with one or more of a company's key commercial processes and with the related frameworks and tools. (An obvious example is brand management.) Companies hoping to operate in a consistent, coordinated way need to define these roles carefully, to fill them with people of the right caliber, and to build a pipeline of talent for the future.

When trying to upgrade the skills of the people occupying pivotal roles, companies often fall into either of two camps. In one are corporations vainly trying to fill their gaps by recruiting a guru or two, often from other industries, such as consumer products. In the other are those hoping, and frequently failing, to train their way to greatness. Many companies need a combination of hiring and nurturing internal talent. From the outside, these companies must find enough talent to achieve the critical mass required for modifying some of their current habits. At the same time, they need leading-edge human-resource and training processes that spot, create opportunities for, and groom internal talent. A leading indicator of success is the ability of marketing executives to move people easily between pivotal roles without missing a beat.

Metrics and performance management

Since what you measure is what you get, it's impossible to put in place an effective operating system without overhauling performance management. To permit useful comparisons of performance for different brands, accounts, and regions, companies need a relatively small number of metrics that are well aligned with business objectives, remain consistent within functions, and can be aggregated across the organization.

Some companies make the common mistake of overhauling their metrics without changing their overall performance-management process. A well-functioning commercial operating system involves frequent, challenging performance reviews during which executives not only assess results but also conduct joint problem-solving and longer-term-development discussions with members of their management teams. Senior executives should always be asking what marketing managers are doing to improve the operating system's core processes and tools so that they remain state of the art.

A beverage company's operating system

To understand how these elements work together in practice, let's return to the beverage company described at the beginning of this chapter. Before the company installed its operating system, it suffered from a host of problems:

- Although the responsibilities of key managers were quite clear ("manage to the budget," "establish and execute on the plan"), they were also fairly narrow. As the company launched more brands toward more and different channels, those narrow, siloed roles began working at cross-purposes.

- The company had six or seven different ways of segmenting customers. As brands proliferated, it became increasingly difficult to determine what customer needs were targeted by various brands, how strong the fit was between brands and target segments, and whether the targeted opportunities were the most attractive ones.

- The company had no systematic way to track the performance of customers, brands, or stock-keeping units (SKUs) across regions and key accounts, so it was difficult to understand the impact of no-frills or private-label brands sold in discount channels.

- Performance measurement was limited. Brand managers focused on measures such as spontaneous and aided awareness, which relate to brand equity and communications programs. Key-account managers primarily emphasized volume.

To address these issues, the company developed a new way of doing marketing and sales—one focused on the brand- and key-account-management processes. At the core of brand management was a new, globally consistent methodology for segmenting customers based on need states (which take into consideration what customers want and how they want it). As part of the new approach, the beverage company gave brand managers tools for understanding which brand attributes contribute most to loyalty in specific segments and for tracking profitability at the segment line.

On the key-account side, the beverage maker built a company-wide "toolbox," which included five analytical methodologies to help key-account teams review account economics, assess customer needs, determine each customer's next-best alternatives, calculate the share of wallet the company was capturing from different segments, and map the decision makers it should influence to deepen its penetration.

To make the new tools work, the company redefined roles in two ways. First, it made brand and key-account managers responsible for interacting frequently with the rest of the organization. Key-account managers, for example, began taking brand positioning into consideration when they set prices and designed promotions, and they worked with plant managers to develop packaging ideas that reduced costs for retail customers. The second, related change was broadening the accountability of brand and key-account managers. The company's new, standard processes helped managers develop brand-, segment-, and customer-level profit-and-loss scorecards. With this information in hand, managers became "mini-CEOs" responsible for both strategic planning and execution in their businesses.

Performance management now reflects the marketing organization's redefined roles. Brand managers augment their old focus on brand equity by emphasizing aggregate performance (measured by the brand's gross margin contribution). Meanwhile, metrics for key-account managers have expanded from volume to profitability and to quality, time, and cost targets that matter to key accounts. By reducing variability and guesswork, the new metrics have dramatically increased the quality of strategic dialogue. Thus, when brand managers present their campaign strategies for the year, they are expected to describe the likely return on different marketing investments, as well as the impact on brand positioning.

With the new level of insight this system provides, corporate marketing can better understand macrotrends within its customer base, identify untapped opportunities, and focus investments on innovation and growth. What's more, the focus on profitability at the brand and key-account levels has made it possible to tie local performance to corporate earnings. Earnings have increased significantly, both because sales to retailers have climbed from 2 to 4 percent in most regions and because aggregate marketing spending declined (by roughly one-fourth) as the operating system eliminated inefficiencies.

In addition to improving financial results, the beverage company's consistent processes, tools, roles, and ways of measuring performance changed the look and feel of marketing. Brand managers communicate with a common language and feel closer to customers because their needs are at the heart of the new approach to segmentation. Sales managers have goals that go beyond closing deals and don't have to go back to the boss as frequently when the need arises for trade-offs. And across sales and marketing, former skeptics like the way the new approach reduces the number of iterations associated with typical tasks.

Ensuring a sufficient focus on core processes and tools

In our experience, fully defining the operating system's central processes and related tools is often a real challenge because they must encompass both rigorous analysis and marketers' creative ideas. The following examples illustrate how two companies defined core aspects of their operating systems and promoted cross-functional linkages—one by using an innovation process, the other by using a profitability tool.

An upgraded innovation process

A manufacturer of consumer durable goods sought to enhance the role of its marketing and sales organization in product innovation as a way to deal with the polarization of its traditional stronghold in the middle-market segments. The company needed to generate more ideas for new products and to ensure that ideas surviving to the concept-development phase were well connected with insights about the wants and needs of consumers. But the innovation process worked in a serial manner: designs for products were nearly finalized before commercialization teams became involved with them. This serial approach inhibited the generation of ideas, hampered the company's ability to fit new products with existing brand strategies, and reduced the effectiveness of product launches. As a result, the company often introduced new products two to three years after nimbler competitors did.

This company responded by redesigning its product-development process and creating a set of tools—including idea generation workshops, in-home observation, and conjoint analysis to highlight key trade-offs—for project leaders to use at each step. It also improved linkages among salespeople (who frequently uncovered important insights about customer needs), pricing and brand managers (whose margin and positioning objectives helped focus research efforts), and members of the R&D group. The company reinforced cross-functional collaboration by establishing checkpoint meetings at each stage of the innovation process (Exhibit 3). The resulting dialogue led to better decisions about whether and how to proceed with new products.

The innovation process itself wasn't groundbreaking. What was significant was the company's use of some relatively straightforward process changes to improve the way different parts of the organization worked together and to ensure that innovation activities fit well with important business objectives. In doing so, the company took a major step toward defining its commercial operating system.

EXHIBIT 3

Avoiding the serial approach

Overview of cross-functional checkpoints along the product-management flow

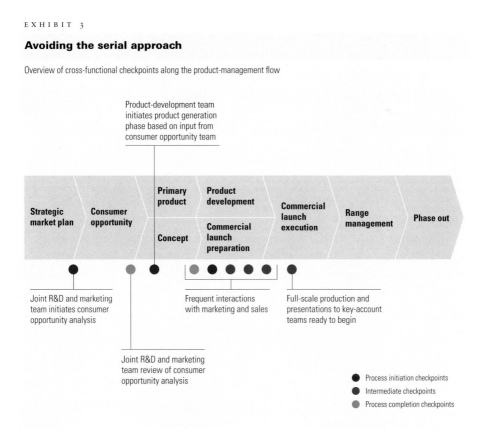

EXHIBIT 4

A tool for salespeople

Relative profitability per customer account, example of specialty-chemical company

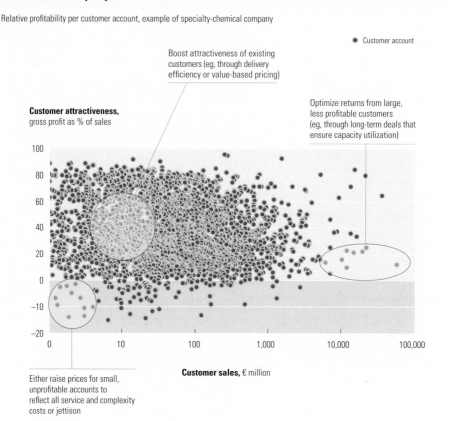

● Customer account

Boost attractiveness of existing
customers (eg, through delivery
efficiency or value-based pricing)

Optimize returns from large,
less profitable customers
(eg, through long-term deals that
ensure capacity utilization)

Customer attractiveness,
gross profit as % of sales

Either raise prices for small,
unprofitable accounts to
reflect all service and complexity
costs or jettison

Customer sales, € million

An account profitability tool

In other instances, analytic tools play an integrating role. A chemical manufacturer sought to upgrade its key-account management because its mid-
tier corporate customer segment was becoming polarized: some customers
valued solutions and high-touch interactions, while others wanted the lowest
possible costs.

The company's improvement efforts featured a new Web-based tool
that enables frontline salespeople to understand the relative profitability
of each account. The tool generates detailed scatter plots that index sales
versus profits by account and customer (Exhibit 4). That information not
only helped salespeople to prioritize accounts but also clarified which level of
service to offer each account.

This tool's importance extended beyond key-account tactics. For starters, by identifying differences in the attractiveness of accounts, the analysis suggested opportunities to improve pricing, thereby enhancing the coordination between pricing and key-account management and bringing greater consistency to both. Furthermore, the tool highlighted the need to develop the skills of certain professionals; salespeople might, for instance, need to negotiate alternative contracts or to define a series of milestones for customers with a limited ability to pay list prices in the short term but great potential for future growth and profitability. Finally, the tool became a key ingredient in performance management.

High-quality processes; leading-edge frameworks and tools; clear responsibilities, skills, and decision-making authority for talent in pivotal roles; and effective performance management represent powerful sources of advantage in a world of proliferation. The consistency, coordination, and insight at the heart of a commercial operating system support excellence in marketing and sales activities ranging from brand and key-account management to the execution and management of pricing, customer segments, and marketing investments.

The authors wish to thank to Joel Claret, Brett Grehan, Thomas Tochtermann, and Catherine Wright for their contributions to this chapter.
•
Trond Riiber Knudsen (trond_riiber_knudsen@mckinsey.com), **Cédric Moret** (cedric_moret@mckinsey.com), and **Evan Van Metre** (evan_van_metre@mckinsey.com) are members of McKinsey's global marketing and sales practice.
Trond Riiber Knudsen is a director in the Oslo office, Cédric Moret is an associate principal in the Geneva office, and Evan Van Metre is a principal in the Atlanta office.

Pricing in a proliferating world

J. Kevin Bright, Dieter Kiewell, and Andrew H. Kincheloe

The exploding number of brands, channels, and distinct customer segments means that many companies must now juggle hundreds of thousands—in some cases, millions—of price points while seeking to maintain consistent pricing strategies and communications across an ever-increasing number of products and outlets. For a broad variety of manufacturers that sell to consumers and businesses alike, this proliferation has made pricing more difficult but the rewards for managing it well much greater.

The proliferation of channels and the microsegmentation of customers have driven the typical consumer packaged goods (CPG) company to create new brands and stock-keeping units (SKUs) as it attempts to limit channel conflict, address unmet needs, and reach for underserved consumption occasions. In extreme cases, some CPG manufacturers with a number of brands and SKUs—selling through various channels at both regular and promotional prices across different geographies—have tried to manage as many as 20 million individual price points each year. In food service, where prices might move on a daily or weekly basis, each transaction may carry a unique price point, elevating the number of pricing decisions to more than 100 million. And sheer transaction volumes aren't the only issue. The introduction of new discount, rebate, and trade allowance categories, combined with customer-specific trade terms negotiated by powerful retailers, has driven down the number of "standard" transactions, further complicating price management.

The environment of business-to-business companies is no less thorny. A leading manufacturer of lighting equipment, for example, manages more than 450,000 SKUs across ten major brands as it tries to meet local market preferences and remain nimble in the face of increasing domestic and overseas competition. Direct-sales representatives, key-account-management teams, and third-party agents sell these products to contractors, local distributors, distribution chains, consortia of small distributors and retailers, and, not least, large home center chains. With more than three million pricing opportunities annually, the challenge of making the right pricing decision every time is enormous.

Traditional models for managing prices are clearly inadequate for these and many other situations. Distributed responsibility for pricing decisions across functions and geographies leaves no one managing the total price-profit-volume equation. Without a common process for making pricing decisions across different brands and channels, as well as a common set of data to support these decisions and monitor performance, pricing becomes unmanageable. The results are inevitable: pricing performance varies enormously among business units, channel conflicts lead major customers to demand price protection, and brand managers compete among themselves for the same consumers and shelf space.

In light of these issues, this chapter doesn't focus on strategies, tactics, or tools for setting prices. Instead, it explores the new operating model many companies need to realize the full potential of today's state-of-the-art approaches to analyzing and improving pricing performance.[1] The model has three characteristics: better visibility into pricing performance and clearer performance standards; a common system for pricing across brands, channels, and segments; and organizational balance, with a central pricing group that integrates the model throughout the company but doesn't make every decision. In many cases, the model will require substantial changes in the way companies make daily pricing decisions, as

---

[1] For a comprehensive treatment of pricing strategies and tactics, see Michael V. Marn, Eric V. Roegner, and Craig C. Zawada, *The Price Advantage*, Hoboken, NJ: John Wiley & Sons, 2004.

well as changes to systems, organizational roles and responsibilities, performance metrics, and incentives. Making these changes stick calls for real dedication and, frequently, a new performance culture focused on pricing.

Visibility into the performance of pricing

For many companies, generating even simple bottom-line price and margin reports for individual customers or SKUs is a monumental task exacerbated by the proliferation of brands, channels, and segments. Companies frequently find themselves with a variety of systems that capture key pricing data. Integrating the data is difficult and time consuming—and therefore rarely done. With so little information available centrally, it isn't surprising that sales forces have even less information when it is most critical—at the point of negotiation. Few companies have tools to help the frontline sales force manage or improve pricing.

This lack of visibility increases the likelihood of wide variations in price points for similar products across disparate channels and customer segments. What's more, the level of discount offered usually isn't related to the size or importance of individual customers, as might be assumed, and raises the risk of channel conflict and arbitrage. In industries ranging from CPG to building products to commodity chemicals, examples abound of very small customers receiving huge discounts and, invariably, of companies serving unprofitable customers. In some cases, the variation among accounts is so significant that companies fear that imposing greater order and structure on frontline pricing could disrupt their business.

Given the importance of incorporating clear information as well as the growing need to bring pricing decisions closer to customers, an integrated database and frontline tools for pricing are essential ingredients of success. Unfortunately, despite the increased sophistication of pricing software, companies still have great difficulty extracting the insights they need to improve their performance in this area. The information required to develop these insights—product volumes, list prices, promotional spending, trade allowances, payment terms, and data on the cost of products, for example—typically resides in a broad array of isolated systems run by finance, sales, logistics, and customer service. At the lighting company mentioned earlier, for instance, managers had to pull data from more than 35 sources to develop a comprehensive profit-and-loss statement for products and customers.

Since compiling and integrating so much disjointed information is a daunting and time-consuming task, it's not surprising that many businesses lack even the most basic insights into profitability at the more granular levels. This failure can prevent the best companies from optimizing their pricing and discount levels. How can you manage pricing when you can't compare net prices across markets or don't know whether a particular price level will leave you with a profit or a loss? Since a 1 percent shift in overall prices can affect profits disproportionately, rules of thumb and gut instinct aren't sufficiently reliable for fine-tuning prices.

Creating transparency

The answer is to combine a laserlike focus on the most important information needed to make pricing decisions with a simple process that integrates this information so that salespeople can use it. One leading beverage company regularly captures and synthesizes accurate field pricing data, including prices, promotions, and shipments at the retail level. This company also enlists its vast field sales forces to calibrate pricing on a market-by-market basis.

By methodically capturing information in a pricing database and support tool, a company creates a consistent set of data to guide its decisions and measure their impact. Both aspects are vital, since visibility and accountability go hand in hand. A Fortune 500 building-products manufacturer, for example, saw that the amounts paid by customers receiving its highest and lowest prices varied by more than 40 percent, even though its products were largely considered commodities. This company faced a common problem: a strong traditional focus on volumes combined with scant pricing data meant that the sales force drove down prices to win deals. Once the company installed a relatively simple software package to integrate its pricing data, it could institute a compensation structure that rewarded gross margin dollars and percentages (in addition to volumes), thereby improving the alignment between the incentives of the sales force and corporate profitability.

After creating visibility, a company must bring this information to bear on decisions. Consider, for example, the very large distribution company that designed a new process its sales reps could use in making on-the-spot pricing decisions. This process not only used discount guidelines that varied by account type, product type, deal size, and geography but also provided for decentralized—though consistent—decisions. To work, however, pricing guidelines for the company's 30,000 products had to be easily accessible to more than 1,000 salespeople. The answer was a relatively simple frontline pricing tool that showed sales reps the range of their pricing authority and displayed historical pricing for the customer at hand as well as recent pricing for comparable accounts.

The pricing tool, supporting interactions between the frontline force and the central pricing group, was a critical link in the new process. Whenever sales reps wanted discounts outside these guidelines, the tool alerted these individuals to forward the deal to the central organization for evaluation. Discounts beyond the guidelines were rarely approved, and competitive pricing data played a key role in evaluating these requests. By centralizing the decision-making process for exceptional cases, the organization minimized unnecessary discounting and reduced the frequency of frontline pricing disparities—including those among separate locations of large national customers—for highly visible SKUs.

Understanding trade spending

Software that makes the impact of trade spending more visible can also improve the performance of pricing. Many CPG manufacturers annually manage hundreds of thousands of individual promotional events or other initiatives across a wide range of retailers, brands, and SKUs. The return on these investments varies a good deal. Usually, it is correlated with some combination of promotional price, duration, frequency, the use of point-of-sale displays and features, geography, customer, product, and time of year. Combining internal shipment and trade-spending information with syndicated store data linked to each event is tedious and time consuming. As a result, most CPG companies measure the performance of only a very small percentage of their events, and even these efforts are inconsistent, since they vary from account manager to account manager.

Some leading packaged goods companies, by contrast, have made the return on their promotional investments a key component of the pricing system. To examine more events, these companies have deployed promotion analysis tools that provide regular and consistent measures of the way events perform. Such tools give the frontline staff immediate feedback that guides future investments. The companies can also review and synthesize their events centrally, which helps them to develop better overall promotional strategies and to allocate funds across brands, channels, and customer segments more effectively.

Institutionalizing core pricing processes

If a lack of visibility makes it difficult to monitor and enforce good pricing, inconsistent processes across an organization further complicate the execution of pricing. As the products and channels of companies become more complex, each silo within an organization develops its own approach to making important pricing decisions, such as pricing new products, negotiating the pricing of deals, and managing trade funds. Without consistency across the organization, a company can't leverage best practices, shift and promote talented workers effectively, or present a uniform image to customers who make purchases in a number of product categories, often from different salespeople.

To ensure consistency across silos over time, it is critical to identify and standardize the two or three most important pricing processes and to institutionalize them across the business. By formally establishing a consistent set of core pricing processes, companies can deploy best practices and process improvements more quickly and make key pricing and promotion decisions more transparent. Other benefits include predictable planning cycles, standardized communications to key retail and distribution partners, and a system of internal checks and balances to avoid poor decisions and potentially illegal pricing actions.

The process problem

The pricing of new products offers a clear example of the challenges generated by the traditional disarray and shows how an embedded pricing process can address them. New brands, products, and packaging have proliferated as companies respond to changing consumer tastes and shifting retail dynamics. Such companies commonly introduce their new products at price points near those of their existing ones, thus cannibalizing the portfolio. Instead of increasing their market share, they divide it among a larger number of SKUs, each competing for the same shelf space, consumer acceptance, and internal resources. Ironically, considering how critical these decisions are, companies often set prices for new products on an ad hoc basis just before they hit the market, with limited or no pricing research to support them.

Manufacturers selling to businesses face an equally profound problem, which frequently stems from introducing new versions of products without effectively retiring the older ones. The net effect is increased inventory costs, greater management complexity, and declining production efficiency.

A major medical-device manufacturer's experience shows some of the problems. This company faced very short product cycles, usually lasting 12 to 18 months. Whenever it launched new versions of a product, it aimed to shift 80 percent of the sales volume to them within 6 months. Yet the company also continued to sell older versions and allowed the sales force to offer deeper discounts to make them attractive to interested customers. These price cuts encouraged such customers to stay with older products. In addition, the company risked dragging down the price of new products, since such heavy discounting could have tarnished the value perception of an entire line. Despite annual R&D investments of hundreds of millions of dollars, the average price for every product line the company offered was declining each year.

Creating consistency

Companies can respond to these challenges by institutionalizing a pricing process for their new products as part of the pricing system. A leading consumer electronics company showed how this can be done in the face of common obstacles. The company sold a range of products targeted at different customer segments that frequently overlapped. Further complicating the picture, each product group had its own manager and its own approach to product pricing, and there was relatively little interaction among silos. To create consistency across the entire organization, the company established a new process—used by all product-management teams—based on four core principles:

1. Pricing must play a role early in the product-development cycle, and any new product must either address a portfolio's gaps (such as price point gaps or underserved segments and channels) or explicitly replace an existing product.

2. New-product introductions represent opportunities to increase prices overall.

3. Whenever possible, product managers must commission research on consumers to understand their price sensitivity and the perceived value of a product relative to competing alternatives.

4. Plans to introduce any replacement product must include a clear strategy for the end-of-life management of the existing one.

These four principles became the centerpiece of a clear process the company could repeat again and again to manage the pricing of new products throughout its portfolio. The process led not only to better pricing decisions for individual products but also to a more cohesive product portfolio, with fewer conflicts and less redundancy.

Pricing new products is just one example of the kind of core pricing processes that companies can standardize across their operating silos. Each company should identify the two or three most critical pricing decisions it faces and focus its efforts on institutionalizing the processes needed to make them. By concentrating investments in process design, training, and support systems on relatively few pricing processes, companies can build capabilities that truly differentiate them from their competitors.

Striking an organizational balance

As companies try to make their pricing performance more visible and to institutionalize core pricing processes, the question of who manages and maintains the infrastructure becomes increasingly important. If most pricing decisions remain decentralized, who makes sure that strategy and tactics are integrated across brands, channels, and segments? Who maintains the central pricing database and mines that data to create reports and identify pricing opportunities? Who trains the organization's people in the elements of the pricing system? Leading companies have answered these questions by creating a central pricing organization—a center of pricing excellence—that maintains basic systems and functions and can collaborate with the rest of the company (exhibit).

To be effective, the pricing organization must be led by a full-time manager who is well respected within the company and has strong interpersonal skills, since the role involves frequent work with sales, marketing, finance, customer service, and operations. While the organization needn't be large to be effective, it must have the ability to perform several key functions. First, it should mine the database and produce regular reports for top managers. Second, the group must collect and synthesize pricing intelligence, which may include consumer research, market studies, and publicly available information about competitors. It may also weigh exceptional discounting requests from frontline sales reps and make recommendations or even final decisions. Last, the organization could be charged with identifying pricing opportunities and leading cross-functional teams to capture them. Whatever its responsibilities, its roles and objectives must be defined clearly.

Collaborating while selectively centralizing

A close look at a case involving a leading consumer electronics manufacturer highlights several key roles for a central pricing group. This company, a leader in a nascent but rapidly growing product category, has fewer than a dozen major products on the market. All have a very short life cycle, and prices can vary widely depending on the sales channel. Each product once had separate managers, as did each of the company's three major channels: distribution, retail, and key accounts. Product managers were responsible for managing the price level and trajectory of their products, and channel managers had relatively unfettered authority to discount products to their customers. The results were predictable: unclear product positioning, cannibalization, significant price variations for individual SKUs, internal tension between sales and product management, and margins that contracted quickly as products matured and were discounted in channels.

EXHIBIT

Integrating pricing strategies

Pricing organization model, selected activities

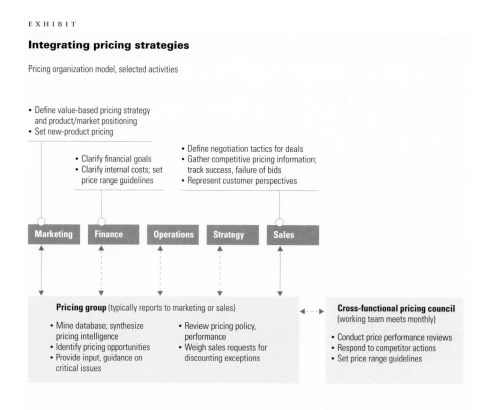

To begin addressing these issues, the company created a pricing organization staffed by a pricing leader and two pricing analysts. The organization's first job was to craft an overall pricing strategy to guide the positioning of the company's products relative to competitive offerings. Next, the organization worked with the consumer insights group to commission external market research, which could be repeated annually, on the entire product portfolio. Of particular importance was the development of price elasticities and cross-elasticities for each product.

After developing this data, the pricing group worked with the product managers to reset prices for the company's entire line. That repositioning alone increased the company's operating margin by more than 20 percent. Then the pricing group took the new price list and developed a set of guidelines and a consistent process for discounting across all channels. In addition, the group developed a set of standard reports that provided the sales force and management with feedback on overall pricing trends, the attainment of prices for each major market and region, competitive pricing dynamics, and the performance of individual products. The net result was a more cohesive and coherent approach to pricing, from top-line strategy to frontline execution.

Coordinating action through a pricing council

More and more, companies are supplementing the pricing organization with a cross-functional pricing council, typically chaired by the pricing leader and including executives from brand, product, sales, and channel management and from customer service, finance, and operations. Meeting every month or two, such a council serves as a central clearinghouse for pricing issues. Among other things, it resolves conflicts across sales and operational silos, refines and coordinates strategy for pricing, reviews the performance of pricing, and responds to major competitive moves. It also identifies broad pricing opportunities—such as across-the-board price increases or the repositioning of the whole portfolio—that cut across multiple brands or channels.

Opportunities to capture value by differentiating prices across proliferating brands, regions, channels, and SKUs are too large to ignore, while the costs of neglecting these opportunities or of trying to address them with piecemeal efforts are substantial. With a new model for price management, companies serving consumers and businesses alike can enhance the role of pricing as a strategic and tactical lever for creating value.

Kevin Bright (kevin_bright@mckinsey.com), **Dieter Kiewell** (dieter_kiewell@mckinsey.com), and **Andy Kincheloe** (andy_kincheloe@mckinsey.com) are members of McKinsey's global marketing and sales practice. Kevin Bright is an associate principal in McKinsey's Toronto office; Dieter Kiewell is a principal in the London office; and Andy Kincheloe is an associate principal in the Atlanta office.

Managing your business as if customer segments matter

**Sean R. Collins, Peter W. Dahlström,
and Marc Singer**

Today's proliferating environment is dramatically increasing the importance of effective customer segment management. Market polarization is widening the gaps between the lifetime values of various segments. Fragmenting customer needs are creating opportunities for specialist competitors to go after just one segment. And proliferating distribution channels and media vehicles are helping all companies target the most valuable customers with focused service and advertising. The result is a powerful need for companies to get better at identifying and delivering distinctive value to their most attractive customer segments.

But few organizations can get their segment strategies to work. Many companies articulate detailed segmentation plans, but they rarely define and manage their segments in a way that helps the organization differentiate the value it offers specific groups of customers. What's more, the planning systems of most companies lack the roles, processes, and integrated customer metrics needed to create unique customer experiences for select segments or to respond quickly to shifts in a segment's value. Indeed, many organizations have difficulty measuring the extent of customer migration (more spending by satisfied customers or less spending by dissatisfied ones)—much less quantifying its financial impact or actively managing it through differentiated customer propositions and experiences.[1] For evidence of this challenge, consider data-rich industries such as financial services, airlines, and retailing, which were among the first to identify meaningfully different segments by parsing large volumes of data. Few companies in these industries have exploited state-of-the-art customer-relationship-management (CRM) technologies to develop and deliver truly differentiated value propositions, create customer-level scorecards, or make them central to running the business. A key reason is that understanding and acting on segment- or customer-level information often requires collaboration among a number of functions that interact with customers across the organization. Facilitating and rewarding such coordination is difficult in product-, service-, and geographically oriented organizations.

In short, developing powerful segmentations—and acting on them by providing distinctive experiences to valuable customers—is much more a management and organizational challenge than one of data, technology, or analytic sophistication. Companies must measure, understand, and focus management attention on what is happening within and across segments, how what is happening there relates to aggregate business or marketing plans, what the implications are for performance management, and which organizational changes are needed to effect segment-level change. More specifically, marketers must complete three tasks:

1. Choose an actionable segmentation, meaning that segment objectives (including customer experience targets) are explicitly linked to overall business goals.

2. Build formal mechanisms within planning, measurement, and performance-management processes to manage customer segments effectively.

3. Create organizational accountability for segment results and empower segment "owners" with the authority to make or influence key decisions.

As we shall see, a few companies—in industries that include retail, telecom, and casino gaming—are leading the way.

---

[1] Many more customers change their spending behavior than defect, so migration frequently accounts for larger changes in value than attrition does. For more on customer migration, see Stephanie Coyles and Timothy C. Gokey, "Customer retention is not enough," *The McKinsey Quarterly*, 2002 Number 2, pp. 80–9 (www.mckinseyquarterly.com/links/20939).

Portrait of the problem

For most companies, periodic (usually monthly or quarterly) reviews of actual performance against the annual plan are critical for determining how best to capitalize on successes and make adjustments for underperformance. Yet in these periodic reviews, most executives don't know what is happening in a number of meaningful segments.

A large retail bank experienced just this problem. The bank planned and tracked performance by product group (such as checking, credit cards, and mortgages) and by channel (including branches, phones, online, and mail). Further, it compared sales, costs, profits, attrition rates, cross-sell penetration, and customer satisfaction across products and channels. But it didn't link performance in individual customer segments—such as investors, retirees, home owners, renters, and students—with aggregate financial objectives and results. Management therefore couldn't pinpoint how strategies to improve customer acquisition, increase penetration, and lower attrition across the bank's key segments were related to the bank's sales and profit goals. Nor was there a process to ensure that the bank modified its tactics as customers moved within and across segments. Finally, given the traditional importance of decentralized product groups and the branch network for developing and sustaining customer relationships, the bank had trouble organizing and managing accountability by customer group instead of along product, channel, and geographic lines.

This situation isn't new. But in a world of proliferation, with rapidly changing segment dynamics, such poor linkages are extremely costly. During a period of rising short-term interest rates, for example, the bank did not understand that a substantial portion of its investor segment was shifting large amounts of short-term liquidity balances to competitors such as ING Direct. Even though these customers reported no changes in satisfaction levels and had no intention of closing their accounts, their annual contribution to the bank's profits fell by 60 to 70 percent. If this institution had understood these dynamics, it might have decided to redesign its products and restructure pricing. But lacking a plan or the ability to measure results along segment lines, the bank did nothing.

Closing the loop

To address this situation, the bank had two needs: first, it had to ensure that its planning and performance-management systems could track and generate prompt reactions to marketplace changes influencing customer acquisition, product or service usage, or attrition rates within and across segments.

Second, it needed a plan that could yield a set of customer proposition and experience initiatives aimed at goals such as increasing usage in the renter segment. With the right level of detail in the metrics, this bank would know exactly how many customers in that segment had increased their usage, how many had decreased it, how many had defected altogether, and what each of these changes was worth.

How could the bank get there? The solution lies in making the approach to segmentation more actionable, linking that approach with the processes for strategy setting and ongoing performance management, and aligning the organization so it can more easily hold individuals and groups accountable for segment-specific sales, profit, retention, and experience targets.

Actionable segmentation

The central challenge of a segmentation strategy isn't how to develop one—a variety of approaches work—but how to make it useful and integrate it into a company's ongoing planning and performance-management efforts. The segmentation must explicitly link corporate financial objectives to the behavior of people in a segment and to customer experience goals. This linkage allows general managers and marketers to understand how the experiences of valued customers influence behavior and how behavioral shifts drive core product or service objectives. It also provides predictive (as opposed to static) measures of customer profitability.

While this is not a particularly technical challenge, the chosen segmentation should meet some important criteria:

- the ability to assign all customers to a segment for an overall line of business, usually defined by a distinct set of common customers, shared channels, and multiple products or services (typically, five to eight primary segments for a business thus defined)

- distinct differences between segments, at least by their current and potential value to the company and by customer behavior and needs

- a clear relationship between these segments and alternative segmentation approaches (such as demographic or attitudinal ones) that are used for various marketing and other purposes (including risk management)

Although nearly all companies have undertaken some version of this process, even those with highly analytical segmentations often have a number of versions for different product groups, geographies, and operating units. Executives hoping to implement company-wide segment-based strategies need to establish a common language for talking about customers across the business. The CEO, for example, should expect product group managers to describe their plans and actual results in common terms across segments, regardless of channel or geography. Only then can the segmentation broadly influence a company's product mix, go-to-market model, brand, and service model or serve as the basis for allocating and prioritizing resources.

Planning processes, metrics, and performance management

Given the complexity of today's marketing environment, the last thing most organizations need is new, independent strategy and planning processes for customer segments. Instead, companies should revamp existing planning exercises so that they become a vehicle for sharing information and for deciding how to go after segment-level opportunities that require collaboration across the organization.

To keep this process manageable, companies should augment traditional mechanisms for defining strategic objectives by adding segment-based P&Ls and operating metrics consistent with aggregate goals. A top-down goal to establish 20 percent market share and a 10 percent earnings before interest, taxes, depreciation, and amortization (EBITDA) margin for a new product, for example, could tie into a segment scorecard with targets for customer acquisition, churn, pricing, and service costs. When corporate financial objectives are explicitly linked to segment-level scorecards, companies can ensure transparency and accountability for segment performance.

Aligning the organization and the segment strategy

With a strategic segmentation defined and clear segment objectives established, companies must clarify the primary locus of customer segment ownership. Segment owners should augment rather than replace the organization's product, service, and functional units and be held accountable for segment-level results.

Companies can either create a new role within a product group or a channel organization or constitute a new segment group that complements existing organizations. Whichever model a company chooses, it must give the segment owners meaningful control over resources and decisions affecting the factors that drive customer experience, corresponding behavior, and segment migration. Examples might include funds specifically for new customer acquisition programs, call-center queues with specialized reps to prevent churn, and personalized online campaigns.

From theory to practice

The experiences of four companies in different industries—casino gaming, luxury retail, and telecommunications (integrated and mobile)—highlight different approaches to capturing value from segment management, as well as some common characteristics. In all cases, the companies succeeded in targeting and actively managing just a few metrics tied to core financial and customer experience objectives. Clear primary ownership and accountability for the results of segment-based changes were the keys to effectiveness.

Case study 1: Casino gaming

A major gaming company faced tough competition and fickle customers. It had a weak loyalty program that based its rewards to customers on their average spending levels but did not factor in how frequently and recently they visited or how much they spent at the casino as a share of their total entertainment expenditures.

The gaming company gradually recognized that tracking average spending gave an inaccurate picture of a segment's potential, because many high-value customers visited competing gaming sites and had outlays that varied significantly over time. Instead, the company decided to track spending flows and to build predictive models based on gaming behavior. As part of the overall segmentation approach, the company established 90 different behavioral segments, each with its own per-visit profit-and-loss forecast.

This segmentation highlighted the need to provide different experiences for customers of different value (Exhibit 1). The casino operator also created a three-tier loyalty program providing differentiated incentives for customers to spend more. To make the change stick, the company created vice presidencies of marketing for each operating division and made the VPs accountable for carrying out the new segment strategy. The executives, in turn, held individual casinos accountable by tightly managing a set of local metrics that allowed properties and specific groups within those properties to measure operational results and to understand their impact upon financial performance.

Each property, for example, had a detailed segment-level scorecard including the number of customers, average revenue per visit, and comparative

EXHIBIT I

Tailored marketing

Disguised example of leading gaming company

Customer experience packages

Type of benefit	Low value	High value
Travel	Free shuttle from airport	Flight to Las Vegas
Hotel room	Discounted rate for standard guest room	3 free nights in luxury suite
Food and drink	Free lunch buffet	Dinner for 2 at steak restaurant
Cash, match play	"Play $5, get $5"	$50–$75 in cash or match play coupons
Shows, activities	None	4 front-row seats to evening show, round of golf at best local course

revenue versus prior visits—metrics that were tied to the property's overall revenue objective. Furthermore, using predictive modeling the company actively tracked the migration of customers, particularly those on the cusp of upward or downward migration. In the end, the company's integrated set of initiatives generated a 25 percent increase in the annual revenue contribution of high-value customers, a 40 percent rise in the number of their visits, and an increase of six percentage points in the casino's share of their entertainment wallets.

Case study 2: Luxury retailer

A high-end retailer with aggressive growth goals decided to delve deeply into the needs and migration patterns of customers who resembled its highest-value customers but spent less. This effort allowed the company to identify several segments that were relatively underpenetrated but had high spending potential and appeared to be interested in the merchandise authority and store experience that were central to the retailer's value proposition. A particularly important segment turned out to be busy professionals seeking fashion and quality.

The company recognized that to increase its wallet share in the target segments, it would have to adapt both its merchandise and the service in its stores to these consumers' distinct need for fashion, quality, and convenience—especially the need to get in and out of stores quickly. But several obstacles stood in the way of taking such steps. For starters, few store managers embraced the complications of identifying and providing differentiated service to specific shoppers. Moreover, the retailer's traditional planning processes took place in silos within marketing, merchandising, and stores, leaving little room for cross-functional segment goals.

To address these issues, the retailer appointed senior executives from merchandising and operations to build new programs and drive execution within existing stores. These executives began by focusing on initiatives designed to increase convenience. In many cases, they charged individual store personnel with targeting customers in the busy, fashion-conscious professional segment.

In addition, the company created a new set of financial and segment-level metrics to track success. After establishing top-down financial targets, the retailer defined segment-specific objectives, such as frequency of visits, incremental sales versus the prior quarter, the number of customers by segment, and cross-sell rates. The retailer also reviewed these new metrics during its regular performance-management meetings with store managers. This integrated, segment-based approach (Exhibit 2)—combining programs aimed at specific customers, segment-oriented planning and performance management, and support for organizational changes—contributed to increases in average spending by target segments: 10 percent growth for all purchases and 30 percent for targeted merchandise categories.

EXHIBIT 2

Targeting segments

Integrated, segment-based approach (fashion retail example)

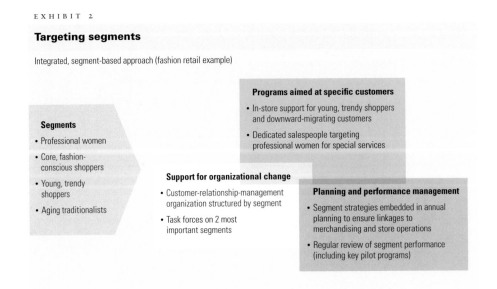

Segments
- Professional women
- Core, fashion-conscious shoppers
- Young, trendy shoppers
- Aging traditionalists

Programs aimed at specific customers
- In-store support for young, trendy shoppers and downward-migrating customers
- Dedicated salespeople targeting professional women for special services

Support for organizational change
- Customer-relationship-management organization structured by segment
- Task forces on 2 most important segments

Planning and performance management
- Segment strategies embedded in annual planning to ensure linkages to merchandising and store operations
- Regular review of segment performance (including key pilot programs)

Case study 3: Integrated telecommunications carrier

A North American telecommunications carrier with wireline, video, voice, and data offerings decided to take an integrated view of its products. One reason was that customers increasingly were purchasing services in bundles from telecom players and cable television operators. Also, the more products customers had, the less likely they were to defect.

The company somewhat differentiated its treatment for customers who were major consumers of a specific service—for example, by giving them their own call-center waiting queues for that service. But it had difficulty identifying the most valuable segments across product groups, much less the best opportunities to deepen penetration, pull off "up-selling," and avoid churn within those segments. The telecom provider knew that improving its effectiveness required a better understanding of the factors shaping customer behavior. It therefore segmented its customers by lifetime value (margins across all products per household) and risk to defect (measured by wireline spending, whether cable was in the area, the number of products held, and a predictive churn model with dozens of service variables, such as whether a customer had multiple recent service calls).

It turned out that two key metrics—the number of households with multiple products and the number of high-value, high-risk households targeted—provided enough insight to integrate segment performance with overall financial goals (Exhibit 3, on the next page). The marketing organization used separate scorecards to track the subdrivers of these two key metrics. Key scorecard measures included the percentage of marketing spending allocated to targeted households, the percentage of customers at risk for attrition who were "saved," and the penetration of the company's services within each account.

The telecom player's CEO created an integrated marketing function intended to generate household-level programs that cut across individual product lines. Tasked with improving acquisition rates, stimulating upward migration, and reducing churn, the group developed new product bundles, coordinated decisions around marketing offers and pricing, and launched initiatives to improve service issues correlated with churn. The company, for example, targeted for retention those customers who had recently disconnected their high-speed data service, because analysis showed that these people were ten times more likely than the average customer to disconnect their fixed-line service within 60 days. As a result of segment-level actions, the company realized improvements in churn, product

EXHIBIT 3

Whom do you target?

Disguised telecom example

xx Thousands of households	Big spenders
$xx Annual profit per household	High potential
	Traditional

	Low	Medium	High	Low	Medium	High
Product bundle A	**150** $60	**100** $150	**80** $250	**70** $170	**60** $200	**50** $400
Product bundle B	**95** $60	**50** $90	**30** $200	**20** $80	**25** $100	**20** $500
Product bundle C	**35** $30	**20** $50	**10** $190	**10** $30	**10** $90	**5** $250
Annual spending by household	Low	Medium	High	Low	Medium	High
	Medium risk to defect			**High risk to defect**		

penetration, and average revenue per user that together helped boost profitability by more than $100 million.

Case study 4: Mobile-telecommunications provider

A European mobile provider sought to attract new customers by enhancing its brand and service propositions. The company assessed all of its customers' value, service needs, and willingness to pay. Historically, the company, like most of its competitors, had focused on brand-loyal, full-service customers. But it quickly identified a relatively large (25 to 30 percent of all customers) and underserved segment of no-frills customers who were very happy to trade the ability to shop in retail stores, call into customer service centers, receive handset upgrades, and see their service provider in TV commercials for a price discount of 20 to 25 percent.

Since the entire front-end service proposition had to be completely different from the core business, the operator decided to set up a separate no-frills business unit whose management team had an equity stake. The company even went so far as to launch a distinct brand for the new unit. Although initially there was strong resistance to organizational separation, it proved critical in achieving the cost structure, operating speed, entrepreneurial culture, and incentives needed to build this type of business from scratch. Over roughly two years, the no-frills unit gained a 10 percent market share.

These examples show how a diverse set of initiatives—offering high rollers free flights to Las Vegas, aiming high-touch service at certain shoppers upon their arrival in stores, launching an entirely new wireless service—can dramatically alter the experiences of targeted segments and produce significant financial gains. As these examples also emphasize, effective customer segment management is easy to talk about but challenging to execute. In fact, that's precisely why it is a powerful basis for sustainable competitive differentiation.

The early leaders have adopted common, actionable segmentation across the entire business, integrated the setting of goals for segment-level customer experiences and financial performance into their planning and performance-management efforts, and established clear organizational accountability for segment-level results. To succeed, they must artfully integrate this approach into the organization's existing product, channel, and geographic orientation in a way that makes a real difference. Taking the plunge is worthwhile because it enables a company to create more valuable relationships with customers.

The authors would like to thank Ewan Duncan and Catherine Wright
for their contributions to this chapter.

•

Sean Collins (sean_collins@mckinsey.com),
Peter Dahlström (peter_dahlstrom@mckinsey.com), and **Marc Singer**
(marc_singer@mckinsey.com) are members of McKinsey's
global marketing and sales practice. Sean Collins is a consultant in McKinsey's Pacific Northwest
office, Peter Dahlström is a principal in the Copenhagen office, and Marc Singer
is a director in the San Francisco office.

Boosting returns on marketing investment

David C. Court, Jonathan W. Gordon, and Jesko Perrey

Today's CMOs confront a painful reality: their traditional model for reaching customers is being challenged, and they can forsee a day when it will no longer work.

The declining effectiveness of mass advertising is only the most visible sign of distress in the marketing world. Marketers also face a general proliferation of media and distribution channels, declining trust in advertising, multitasking by consumers, and digital technologies that give users more control over their media time.[1] These trends are simultaneously fragmenting audiences and the channels needed to reach them. At best, marketers can expect that the time-honored way of getting messages to consumers through traditional media such as broadcast television will be rendered less effective. At worst, advertising in these media will become a waste of time and money. This danger is accompanied by the challenges of proliferation in the scale and scope of marketing—for instance, the growing number of brands in most industries and companies—and in the internal and external people required for marketing efforts, not to mention the variety of skills and measurement approaches they need.

---

[1] Michael P. Zeisser, "Marketing in a post-TiVo world," *The McKinsey Quarterly*, 2002 special edition: Technology after the bubble, pp. 89–92 (www.mckinseyquarterly.com/links/20938).

Among marketers, there's much frustration and little agreement about what to do next. Some are reaching for marketing-mix models that use sophisticated econometric methods to tease out the different effects of the marketing mix on business results (see sidebar "Beware the quantitative cure-all"). But the historical data that fuel such techniques may prove an unreliable guide to future returns.

To understand their fragmenting world, marketers need a more rigorous approach—one that jettisons mentalities and behavior from advertising's golden age and treats marketing not as spend but as the investment it really is. In other words, it will be necessary to boost marketing's return on investment (ROI). By adhering to the same investment principles that other functions follow, a chief marketing officer (CMO) can improve the alignment between marketing and financial objectives, capitalize on a brand's most distinctive elements with greater success, more precisely target the customers and communication vehicles yielding the largest and fastest payoff, manage risk more carefully, and track returns more closely. In short, CMOs hoping to master their proliferating environment must thoughtfully and systematically apply investment fundamentals to marketing planning and performance management.

Beware the quantitative cure-all

Some companies wonder if marketing-mix models or marketing ROI systems are the antidote to the bewildering complexity of today's marketing environment. These analytic techniques, which have been around for years, seem to provide exactly what marketers are looking for: sophisticated insights into the relative importance of different media channels. Indeed, when consumer decision processes, media channels, and basic model parameters are stable, such models work well. We have seen them take in reams of data and complex inputs—weights of mass media, copy-effectiveness scores, relative pricing levels, store-level execution variables, and even weather reports—and provide insightful perspectives on issues facing the underlying business or valuable contributions to the budget-setting process.

Yet savvy marketers have long known that the strength of marketing-mix modeling—a rigorous

analytical assessment of the past—is also its Achilles' heel when it is applied to situations where important changes are under way. Take, for instance, the automotive industry (where the Internet is transforming decision-making processes) or packaged goods (where indirect-marketing approaches, such as product placements, are gaining importance for many brands). In situations such as these, marketing-mix models may provide unreliable forecasts.

Relying on such models without first broadly rethinking marketing investments also raises another problem: right or wrong, these models may inspire blind faith in analytic results. In our experience, boosting marketing returns cannot be only about getting the numbers. It must start with an understanding of the brand as a holistic economic entity and extend to the way a marketing department does business.

The ROI challenge

Today's ROI challenge has its roots in the halcyon days of mass advertising, in the 1960s and '70s. Back then, marketers wrote the rules that still inspire many marketing investments—or, as some tellingly say, marketing spend.

Legacy issues . . .

When network television was king, marketers and the ad agencies serving them rightly focused on the massive audiences that tuned into the most popular shows. The emphasis was on "mass messaging": the development of powerful advertisements imprinting themselves on the minds of consumers. Many marketers based their TV spending on "share of voice," which meant making sure that a brand's advertising budget was in line with its market share, the spending of competitors, and the company's growth expectations. Plans for other media expenditures received less attention. Share of voice also predominated in some business-to-business (B2B) industries, and in pharmaceuticals, where the emphasis was largely on influencing physicians with marketing pitches delivered by sales representatives.

Golden-age marketers often relied on tools such as day-after recall, a metric tracking how well customers remember ads. To assess the effectiveness of ad copy, they compared these results with internal benchmarks. As it became clear that recall wasn't the best measure of creative effectiveness, leading companies developed more elaborate testing regimens, such as the audience response system (ARS), a technique for determining the persuasive impact of new messages as compared with those of competitors. Meanwhile, more precise reach and frequency assessments made media-spending decisions better informed.

While the model worked extremely well for consumer product companies such as Coca-Cola, Colgate-Palmolive, and Unilever, it wasn't perfect. Share-of-voice thinking and up-front media buys can create considerable inertia about spending. What's more, the runaway success of TV-driven brand building meant that many marketers never really had to justify their budgets or to develop metrics that made sense to businesspeople elsewhere in the organization. Basically, marketers dealt with the ROI issue through a combination of practical experience and rules of thumb. Indeed, the absence of consensus on how to define—much less measure—returns on marketing investments sometimes challenged marketers' credibility.

Nonetheless, in a world of largely captive audiences, effective messaging, consistent consumer behavior, and well-understood competition, the approaches perfected during the golden age worked efficiently. They established priorities, managed risk, and measured the impact of spending on consumer attitudes. Indeed, the model worked so well that during the 1980s and '90s, companies in pharmaceuticals, retailing, telecommunications, and other industries began recruiting marketers from packaged-goods leaders and adopting their techniques.

. . . exposed by a changing market

Fragmenting media and changing consumer behavior are exposing the limits of the traditional model. Consider the following trends.

- *Media proliferation.* In the United States, the original handful of TV stations has proliferated into more than 1,600 broadcast and cable TV outlets. Similar trends are under way in Europe.

- *Multitasking.* While surfing the Web, the typical US teenager engages in an average of two other activities, one of which is often homework (Exhibit 1). Some 80 percent of businesspeople also multitask.

- *"Switching off."* Consumers are increasingly selective about what they watch and the advertising messages they trust. According to Yankelovich Partners, 65 percent of them feel "constantly bombarded

EXHIBIT 1

Fragmented attention

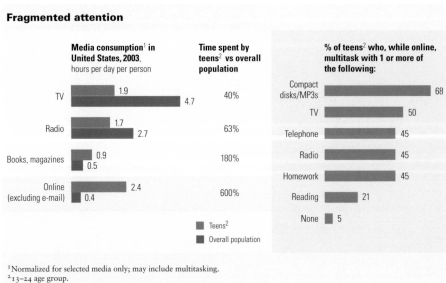

[1] Normalized for selected media only; may include multitasking.
[2] 13–24 age group.

Source: BIGresearch; Veronis Suhler Stevenson; McKinsey analysis

with too much advertising," 69 percent are "interested in products and services that would help skip or block marketing," and 54 percent "avoid buying products that overwhelm with advertising and marketing."

By 2010, we estimate, television advertising in the United States could be only 35 percent as effective for some as it was in 1990. Many European countries are likely headed down a similar path. And while the impact of recent trends on B2B marketing is harder to measure, it probably will be similarly dramatic as common marketing vehicles (such as direct mail, sponsorship events, trade magazines, and sales forces) become less effective.

Although television in some form will remain a formidable medium for many years to come, marketers of all stripes will also have to interact with customers in novel ways by focusing more on new media (such as rich-content Internet marketing and viral marketing) and mastering an environment where messages have to "pull" customers. Compounding matters for marketers is proliferation in the number of marketing-oriented industries, such as pharmaceuticals and mobile telephony; the number of brands and subbrands; and the objectives tied to any given investment—not just long-term brand building but also, for example, improving pricing, boosting sales force effectiveness, and enhancing corporate image.

Setting goals, developing messages, and measuring results have therefore become more difficult. Marketing expenditures come in an ever-expanding variety of flavors, each with different target segments, payback horizons, and metrics for success. These differences make it harder to follow old budgeting rules of thumb, to focus messages on building mass awareness or loyalty, to optimize spending across a portfolio of brands, and to identify the segments or countries most responsive to different marketing initiatives. As customers become increasingly difficult and costly to reach, it becomes still harder to track the way they receive messages. At the same time, many marketers have observed a declining level of discipline in the way companies test the potential impact of advertising (along with other forms of communication) and review its actual impact. Some think that in today's fragmented environment, it has become more difficult to measure the impact of marketing programs on jaded consumers. Others suggest that marketing units are too busy delivering messages across proliferating media channels to conduct campaign postmortems.

Although marketers know about these problems, the marketing industry—whose wide-ranging participants include ad agencies, media companies, research providers, and marketers themselves—has adjusted

EXHIBIT 2

What's wrong with this picture?

Prime-time TV[1] in United States

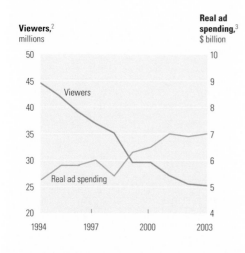

Viewers,[2]
millions

Real ad
spending,[3]
$ billion

[1] Segment of broadcast day from 8 PM–10 PM; includes 4 major networks (ABC, CBS, Fox, NBC).
[2] Estimated.
[3] Adjusted for inflation to 2004 dollars.
Source: Deutsche Bank; *TV Program Investor*, Kagan Research

slowly. Real spending on prime-time television ads, for example, has continued to rise, even as the number of viewers has plummeted (Exhibit 2). These trends are typified by the spending patterns of US automakers, which increased their marketing expenditures per car during the 1990s even as advertising became less effective and their collective market share declined. At the 2004 meeting of the American Association of Advertising Agencies, Jim Stengel, P&G's global marketing officer, said, "I believe today's marketing model is broken. We're applying antiquated thinking and work systems to a new world of possibilities."[2] Some companies have tried responding—through steps such as engaging new agencies (such as online, viral, and ethnic-marketing specialists), attempting new measurement approaches (such as media-specific measurement systems), and involving new stakeholders (such as finance organizations, which are getting more worried about returns on marketing dollars). But ironically, these efforts often wind up adding even greater complexity to the mix.

How marketers should respond

It's time for marketers to be consistent in applying investment fundamentals— such as clarifying the objectives of investments, finding and exploiting points of economic leverage, managing risk, and tracking returns—that have long been well established elsewhere in companies. Such principles of investment management, applied to the marketing function, can create a coherent overview of a company's entire marketing outlay at a time of splintering audiences and communication vehicles, while helping to overcome inertia in spending patterns. When marketers follow these principles,

[2] Ken Auletta, "The new pitch," *New Yorker*, March 28, 2005.

they are better able to make specific interventions at the points of economic leverage where returns on investment are highest, thereby mitigating the dilutive effect of a fragmenting environment and helping to resolve the tension created by the declining efficacy of traditional media vehicles and the subscale nature of emerging alternatives.

Smart marketers won't apply the principles blindly. Translating them to the marketing function calls for a subtle sense of the marketer's art.

Clarify investment objectives

Good financial advisers start by asking clients about their investment horizons, growth expectations, and appetite for risk. Marketing investments should start with similar questions. Answering them helps align the goals of marketers with those of the company as a whole—essential if marketing is to be reconnected to broader business objectives. For example, if company objectives require growth in contiguous businesses, marketing must help more people accept the brand and expand its relevance to a broader set of products. IBM has shown the way by extending its brand through a consistent association with "e-business."

To address the increasingly acute problem of how to optimize a number of investments, each with different time horizons and measures of success, across brands and media channels, it's also vital to distinguish between "maintenance" and "growth" objectives for different segments and media channels. By maintenance, we mean the minimum spending that is required for a competitive presence in the marketplace. Competitive spending levels, S-curve analyses, and purchase cycles help determine appropriate levels of market expenditure. By growth, we mean investments to increase a brand's market share, drive incremental consumption, or attract new users to a category.

Although differentiating between these two types of investments can be tricky, the discipline involved in attempting to do so typically promotes a valuable internal dialogue that helps CMOs impose economic discipline and make trade-offs among brands, markets, and geographies. Over time, savvy marketers get better at categorizing investments, identifying the right maintenance levels for different categories, and allocating growth investments to the products and markets where they will yield the highest returns.

Find new points of economic leverage

For CEOs, the key to economic leverage is allocating capital to the businesses generating the highest returns. For marketers, economic leverage comes from aligning messages and spending with a brand's most compelling elements. In this way, marketers more precisely target their message to the consumers and vehicles providing the biggest and fastest payoff—an essential task as media channels and segments proliferate. Finding and exploiting economic leverage helps marketers know how much it is worth to increase brand awareness as compared with brand loyalty and which segments are most profitable and most responsive to marketing programs at which stages of the consumer decision funnel.

There are two, often complementary, keys to achieving this result. One is to identify the drivers of a company's brands and determine the implications of those drivers for messaging to customers. The other is to examine in detail the reach, cost, and quality of competing investment options and to set marketing priorities accordingly.

First consider brand drivers, which are the critical factors that influence a brand's image and consumer loyalty and that, if improved, increase revenues and profits. In an image-driven business, such as beer targeted at young men, the brand driver could be, "This brand is irreverent" or "I like to drink this brand when I am with friends." In a more transactional business, such as retailing, it could be, "I get good service" or "I found what I wanted."

Most marketers understand their brands' drivers, but few marketers use these drivers rigorously enough to manage multimedia programs, nor do they assess the influence of particular drivers on specific customer segments at various points across the consumer decision funnel. Fortunately, proven analytic techniques, such as structural equation or pathway modeling, can help marketers assess the historical outcome of specific programs to enhance brand drivers over time.[3] In fact, brand drivers can be an integrated metric for determining whether a brand's media and message are effective and in line with the company's strategy.

During the 1990s, a marketer that relied heavily on sports sponsorships faced a big increase in the cost of its contracts. The company had to choose between massive spending increases or the risky step of streamlining its sponsorship portfolio. Using the pathways approach, the company identified the sponsorships that best communicated its core brand drivers. With this knowledge, it focused its dollars on owning and exploiting a specific set of sponsorships, which helped the company maintain near-double-digit growth.

---

[3] Pathway modeling applies a type of multivariate statistical analysis (known as pathway analysis or structural equation modeling) to quantify relationships between brand benefits and product attributes. For details, see Nora A. Aufreiter, David Elzinga, and Jonathan W. Gordon, "Better branding," *The McKinsey Quarterly*, 2003 Number 4, pp. 28–39 (www.mckinseyquarterly.com/links/21112).

It's possible to go a step further and complement brand driver analysis with additional tools that, together, yield a holistic approach for optimizing marketing investments across a broad variety of media. To understand how, consider the global car manufacturer that sought, in an increasingly complex segment, channel, and media environment, to strengthen its brand while boosting growth and profitability. The company initially focused on understanding bottlenecks in the decision funnel for each of its customer segments. Studies show that consumers move through the purchase process predictably—from awareness to familiarity to consideration to the test-drive and, finally, to the purchase—with new requirements on the brand at every stage of the selection process.[4] The funnel method helped the company realize it was overspending at the purchase stage (at the dealerships) while underspending on mass advertising to build awareness. However, this method was not precise enough to show how to optimize marketing investments by segment, brand, and model at each stage in the funnel.

To accomplish this goal, the company developed a methodology for combining measures of reach (the number of unique, relevant customers who are actually exposed to the message), cost (the actual cost to reach 1,000 such customers), and quality (the relative quality of various marketing and trade activities), which allowed it to understand the trade-offs between different investment choices. For one of its models, the automaker wanted to invest in ways to move consumers along the purchasing funnel from familiarity to trial (a test-drive). By combining standard measures of reach and cost with quality factors such as the length, interactivity, credibility, and emotional strength of 16 different media types, the company arrived at the real cost of engaging customers through each medium. Similarly, Exhibit 3, on the next page, shows the results of an analysis of real cost per qualified contact, in this case conducted by a maker of consumer products. Companies using such an approach sometimes find they are getting less bang for their buck through traditional media (such as TV advertising) than with a targeted instrument—for example, appearances at auto shows.

The auto manufacturer still uses the funnel to determine where its message will have the biggest impact. It also still employs brand driver analysis to determine the type of message that will resonate most with each customer segment. And the addition of the reach-cost-quality methodology has allowed it to allocate marketing funds more precisely. Early

---

[4] For more on consumer decision funnels in the automotive sector, see Anjan Chatterjee, Matthew E. Jauchius, Hans-Werner Kaas, and Aurobind Satpathy, "Revving up auto branding," *The McKinsey Quarterly*, 2002 Number 1, pp. 134–43 (www.mckinseyquarterly.com/links/20935).

EXHIBIT 3

Reach, cost, and quality

True cost[1] to contact category users to encourage trial (disguised example of company),
$ per 1,000 unique consumers

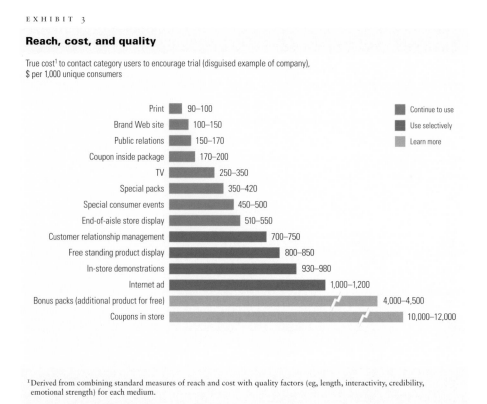

▉	Continue to use
▉	Use selectively
▉	Learn more

Print   90–100
Brand Web site   100–150
Public relations   150–170
Coupon inside package   170–200
TV   250–350
Special packs   350–420
Special consumer events   450–500
End-of-aisle store display   510–550
Customer relationship management   700–750
Free standing product display   800–850
In-store demonstrations   930–980
Internet ad   1,000–1,200
Bonus packs (additional product for free)   4,000–4,500
Coupons in store   10,000–12,000

[1] Derived from combining standard measures of reach and cost with quality factors (eg, length, interactivity, credibility, emotional strength) for each medium.

results suggest that the new approach, while imperfect, is helping the company make better apples-to-apples comparisons across a wide range of media choices, influence customers more effectively, and save money on marketing investments.

Manage investment risk

It's difficult to boost returns in financial markets without assuming additional risk. But for most businesses, selectively reducing risk is one of the critical elements of improving the return on investments; a savvy strategist, for example, minimizes risks by staging them.

Marketing risks were smaller when the media environment was more stable, but marketers now must use similar tactics to keep risks in line. Often, as much as 20 to 25 percent of spending should finance well-structured experiments in communication vehicles (such as digital media, cell phones, viral marketing, and DVDs) that consumers seem less likely to "switch off."

In fact, our experience suggests that one of the best ways to diagnose a marketing organization's ROI discipline is to assess the extent and quality of the media and messaging tests in progress at any given time. Some will be simple, such as testing higher levels of expenditure or new media for a proven message, reducing the frequency of mailings to see if response rates change, and testing a new advertising message in a particular region. Others, such as a simultaneous test of a new message and new media for a growing segment of profitable customers, are bigger departures from the routine. (For more on new media, see sidebar "The promise of digital advertising," on the next page.) Marketers who skimp on experimentation may be overtaken by changing media patterns or forced to assume large risks by rolling the dice on unproven programs when markets shift. Upstart brands such as Red Bull have demonstrated the power of alternative approaches by successfully building consumer awareness through trade promotions, sponsorships, and word of mouth.

Fruitful as tests and new communication methods can be, shifting the bulk of an established marketing plan to them is too risky, because none of the approaches has achieved the scale needed to replace television, radio, direct mail, or other broad-reach media vehicles. So even in today's fragmenting world, marketers should still invest roughly 75 to 80 percent of their money on proven messages (such as advertising copy qualified in research) that are placed in proven media vehicles and supported by proven dollar levels (at or just above the threshold levels needed to influence customers). In these proven programs, managers' key task is to regain the testing and validation discipline that many of them once had.

Track investment returns

The idea that boosting returns on investment depends on measuring them carefully might appear simplistic, but this approach can be a major departure for companies that take a narrow view of their spending or of their measurement of success.

Formerly, marketers could evaluate just the dollars in their marketing budgets, but it's now vital to consider all of the marketing plan's expenditures, including, at a minimum, all sponsorships, major media, and sales collateral. Many companies should also integrate sales promotion activity and (particularly for retailers, banks, and consumer telecom companies) store-level spending. This is often difficult because of disparate systems and data sources. However, the act of recording total expenditures and the customers targeted by each, even at a relatively high level, can make a big difference. For example, when a leading European mobile-services provider realized

The promise of digital advertising

It's easy to understand the hype that surrounds digital advertising. By some measures, US consumers already spend more time online than in front of the television set, and digital marketing appears to be more cost effective than traditional vehicles. Nonetheless, while marketers should prepare to shift ever larger portions of their spending to digital media over time, they must realize that structural constraints will limit the migration of advertising to the Web in the near term.

More than 35 percent of the US population now has broadband Internet access at home, up from 5 percent in 2000. This figure is expected to grow to 50 percent by 2007. The adoption of broadband affords users the opportunity to participate in more activities online, such as watching video, which in turn drives the consumption of media online. In 2004 online media represented about one-third of all media viewed or experienced—roughly the same proportion as television, and as much as radio, newspapers, and magazines combined.

Early research suggests that digital marketing can be two to five times more cost effective than traditional media in driving impact across the consumer decision funnel. What's more, technological advances (such as new Internet access models and tools to analyze online behavior) seem poised to help media companies profile their users in ever greater detail.

So marketers will continue to spend more online. Our research suggests that, by 2007, those in the United States will devote from 7 to 10 percent ($16 billion to $23 billion) of their measured media spending to digital advertising—up from 5 percent in 2004. Maturing online-marketing vehicles such as search engine ads, banners, and online video ads will account for much of this growth; emerging channels, such as the delivery of ads to cell phones, will also contribute.

Despite the promise, online advertising probably won't challenge the traditional media's leading role in the next few years, for several reasons. First, inventories of many highly effective digital-advertising vehicles (including ads tied to key words that consumers enter when using search engines and online video ads) are or will soon be constrained. As this happens, prices will go up, reducing the cost effectiveness of these media. Second, many traditional ad agencies lack the skill and experience to conduct a digital campaign successfully, which presents the marketers who employ them with the major task of integrating traditional media campaigns with online ones developed by newer, more specialized agencies. Last, the adoption of digital media will be slowed by the absence of a widely accepted independent measure of digital media (such as Nielsen Media Ratings in traditional media). This problem makes it difficult to do apples-to-apples comparisons of advertising using different kinds of media.

These constraints are largely temporary. As online-media companies create more advertising capacity, ad agencies gain experience, and measurement technology evolves, many marketers will be able to shift larger portions of their budgets to digital media. Advertisers should prepare today by building their skills and transforming their marketing organizations to harness the opportunity.

Christopher J. Grosso, Amy G. Shenkan, and Bart Sichel

Chris Grosso (christopher_grosso@mckinsey.com), **Amy Shenkan** (amy_shenkan@mckinsey.com), and **Bart Sichel** (bart_sichel@mckinsey.com) are members of McKinsey's global marketing and sales practice. Chris Grosso and Bart Sichel are associate principals in McKinsey's New York office, and Amy Shenkan is a consultant in the San Francisco office.

that it had unintentionally been focusing too much on its existing customers, this understanding led to changes in the budget process.[5]

Making expenditures transparent is a necessary but insufficient step. While all marketers track their progress, few measure it end to end by following the trail all the way from the effect of spending on a brand's drivers to the influence of those drivers on consumer loyalty and the influence of loyalty on revenues and margins and, finally, to the question of whether any increase in profits justifies the spending. This end-to-end view is necessary for marketers to understand not only the current returns on marketing programs but also, and equally important, why the programs did or didn't work—information needed to improve future returns.

The global auto manufacturer that in an earlier example focused on the reach, cost, and quality of its marketing investments also undertakes periodic benchmarking analyses to assess the impact of investments along each stage of the purchasing funnel. After revamping its media strategy in hopes of boosting the number of customers who test-drive its cars, the company began comparing changes in conversion rates for each of its target customer segments and reviewing, through an analysis of brand drivers, the impact on overall image.

Marketers aiming for strong returns should start seeing themselves as investment managers for their marketing budgets. That may be more difficult and time consuming than relying solely on old rules of thumb or new analytic approaches, but it is the only answer in today's marketing environment.

[5] Hajo Riesenbeck and Jesko Perrey, *Mega-Macht Marke: Erfolg messen, machen, managen*, Heidelberg, Germany: Redline Wirtschaft, 2005.

The authors wish to thank Mauricio Ibanez, Jeff Kaplan, Philippe Mauchard, Bart Sichel, and Alvin Silk for their contributions to this chapter.

•

David Court (david_court@mckinsey.com),
Jonathan Gordon (jonathan_gordon@mckinsey.com), and **Jesko Perrey**
(jesko_perrey@mckinsey.com) are members of McKinsey's global marketing and sales practice.
David Court is a director in McKinsey's Dallas office,
Jonathan Gordon is a principal in the New York office, and Jesko Perrey is a principal
in the Düsseldorf office.

Managing a marketing and sales transformation

Joel Claret, Pierre Mauger, and Eric V. Roegner

The previous chapters describe a marketing environment of unprecedented change and complexity. The result is a need to reorganize brand portfolios, rethink spending approaches, generate more fine-grained customer insights, overhaul pricing and segment management, and restructure sales, service, and channel strategies. Each change is a challenge in its own right, and some companies are tackling more than one: GE, for example, has been trying simultaneously to improve the way it approaches innovation, brand management, and customer care. This level of change represents a *commercial transformation*—that is, a transformation of the company's broad-based marketing and sales elements.

It's difficult to carry off change of this magnitude at a brisk pace: deeply ingrained habits keep employees from embracing new techniques, skill-building efforts break down, and leaders lose focus. To counteract these problems, companies have developed a variety of change-management approaches, particularly in operations, where techniques such as Six Sigma and Total Quality Management (TQM) have flourished. Making change stick typically requires both planning and action—centering change on a powerful aspiration, establishing systems and processes that reinforce the goals of change, modifying mind-sets by creating a sense of shared purpose among employees, conducting targeted skill-building efforts, and creating role models for employees.[1] While such change-management practices are useful, they are difficult to apply to marketing and sales. One reason is that these organizations—encompassing brand managers, market researchers, and segment and channel managers, to name just a few—are more diverse and complex than the shop floors where many improvement programs take place. Figuring out how to keep disparate parts of the organization working together is a key challenge of change. Second, the rationale for transforming a marketing organization is often to jump-start growth. That requires creativity, not just strong execution, so the change effort is more difficult and the related decision making more complex. Finally, the responses of competitors and customers to marketing changes are difficult to predict, so it is hard to eliminate variability (a goal of many operations change efforts); maintaining flexibility is essential; and the establishment of goals and metrics is complicated.

In our experience, five critical ingredients of transformation are key to overcoming these issues (Exhibit 1):

1. *Leadership, aspirations, conviction, and clarity of purpose:* committed leadership that can bring together disparate parts of an organization to achieve an ambitious and clearly articulated aspiration

2. *New ways of working:* a combination of improved processes and tools that help make sense of complex information, redefined pivotal roles, and performance management that drives the transformation forward; together, these serve as the foundation of a *commercial operating system* that, when fully developed, improves consistency, coordination, insight, and decision making

3. *Capability building:* on-the-job apprenticeship and high-caliber coaching designed to upgrade critical skills while delivering results

4. *Changes in mind-sets and behavior:* necessary steps such as removing cultural barriers to change and developing a tailored set of interventions to shape behavior

---

[1] John P. Kotter, "Leading change: Why transformation efforts fail," *Harvard Business Review*, March 1995, Volume 73, Number 2, pp. 59–67; Jonathan D. Day, Emily Lawson, and Keith Leslie, "When reorganization works," *The McKinsey Quarterly*, 2003 special edition: The value in organization, pp. 20–9 (www.mckinseyquarterly.com/links/20648); and Emily Lawson and Colin Price, "The psychology of change management," *The McKinsey Quarterly*, 2003 special edition: The value in organization, pp. 30–41 (www.mckinseyquarterly.com/links/20141).

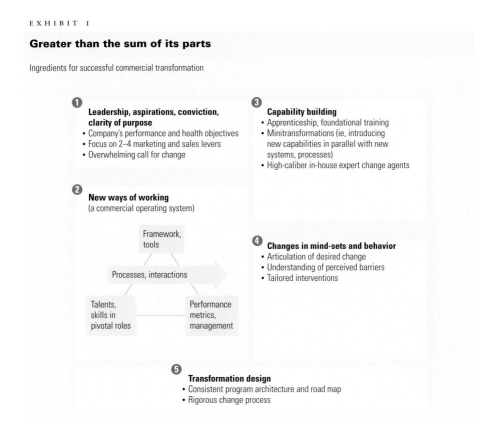

EXHIBIT I

Greater than the sum of its parts

Ingredients for successful commercial transformation

① Leadership, aspirations, conviction, clarity of purpose
- Company's performance and health objectives
- Focus on 2–4 marketing and sales levers
- Overwhelming call for change

② New ways of working
(a commercial operating system)

Framework, tools

Processes, interactions

Talents, skills in pivotal roles

Performance metrics, management

③ Capability building
- Apprenticeship, foundational training
- Minitransformations (ie, introducing new capabilities in parallel with new systems, processes)
- High-caliber in-house expert change agents

④ Changes in mind-sets and behavior
- Articulation of desired change
- Understanding of perceived barriers
- Tailored interventions

⑤ Transformation design
- Consistent program architecture and road map
- Rigorous change process

5. *Transformation design*: an approach that delineates the scope of the journey of change and the support needed to meet its objectives

Focusing on all five priorities at once is a challenge, but in our experience companies that undertake a transformation in a piecemeal fashion risk seeing the effort run off the rails. Executives who pay attention to the marketing- and sales-specific subtleties around each of these levers dramatically increase the odds of successfully overhauling any aspect of the marketing mix, including brand management, channel strategy, pricing, and the way the sales force interacts with customers.

Leadership and aspirations

Achieving this degree of change in marketing and sales presents unique leadership challenges. For starters, performance goals such as boosting revenue can be achieved in many ways: improving customer service, developing new products, raising prices, and more. Further, with so many competitive and customer variables at work, results often take time to appear. Under such conditions maintaining focus is difficult, particularly as opportunities arise. Adding to the complexity of efforts to lead commercial transformations is the great number of interdependencies among, say, brand, key-account, pricing, and service management.

In our experience, most senior executives are surprised to see how much time and energy they have to invest in dealing with these issues in order to clarify the direction of change, maintain leadership focus, and communicate conviction. Consider, for example, a North American retailer that sought to transform itself from a company that served everybody into one that distinctively served its most profitable customer segment. Along the way, management encountered temptations to play in other attractive segments, but succumbing would have undermined the focus of the company's change effort—a broad endeavor that extended to merchandising, store layouts, and backroom operations. Thanks to the CEO's passion and unrelenting focus over a period of years, the company succeeded and overtook many of its competitors. At the other extreme, companies in industries as diverse as chemicals and high tech have mounted sales and marketing change efforts that suffered from the absence of a passionate and visible leader, reliance on a single corporate champion rather than a committed team, or the lack of a well-defined purpose.

Lofty aspirations not only help with focus but also get disparate parts of an organization working together. A case in point is GE's publicly stated goal of achieving organic growth of 8 percent a year—three percentage points higher than the company's historic, acquisition-fueled rates. According to GE, achieving this goal required big ideas that could generate at least $50 million in incremental revenue. Often the only way to develop such ideas is for product developers, brand managers, market researchers, salespeople, and others to pull together across organizational boundaries and business units. As these people come together, the company is identifying growth opportunities while, at the same time, embedding greater consistency in its marketing approaches (such as brand and key-account management) and innovation techniques across regions and businesses.

New ways of working

No multiyear transformation is possible without changing the way people work—the tools they employ, the definition of their roles, and the way their work is measured. Making changes such as these is particularly challenging for marketing and sales organizations. In particular as proliferation boosts the number and complexity of the opportunities that marketers must assess, the sheer variety of the available analytic approaches makes it difficult to choose the core tools and frameworks that professionals should use to improve decision making. Often, companies must redefine roles to get employees out of the traditional functional boxes and to facilitate the integration of insights about customers, intelligence about competitors, and interdependent activities, such as setting prices, developing products, and creating messages. Finally, the development of metrics for tracking progress is challenging because common marketing measures (such as margins, share growth, and sales costs) are sometimes at odds with one another and often require a different emphasis across business units.

Yet the effort associated with putting in place new tools and frameworks yields important benefits. Consider the experience of a packaged-goods company that built a company-wide tool kit to guide key-account planning. The tool kit included five supporting analytical methodologies to help key-account teams review the economics of accounts, assess the needs of customers, determine the next-best alternatives of each, calculate the share of wallet the company captured from different segments in key accounts, and map the decision makers it had to influence to penetrate these accounts more deeply. When every region adopted these standardized tools and templates, the entire organization had a common language to describe how it planned accounts. This achievement facilitated more fact-based decision making about the company's product mix, promotions, trade spending, and service approaches; a clearer view of the trade-offs the company was making; and better comparisons across accounts, brands, and regions.

Even with the right tools in place, marketers must often redefine some roles substantially to ensure that key professionals focus on the right priorities. Two technology companies that changed the way they managed key accounts learned the benefits of properly scoping pivotal roles and the dangers of failing to do so. The first company broadened the roles of the managers in charge of several hundred of its largest accounts to include assembling cross-functional teams of sales support and technical-service people, setting product-specific sales and margin targets, holding business units responsible for sales and product delivery requirements, and seeking profitable opportunities to meet its customers' need for new applications. The second company, in contrast, didn't empower its managers to develop customer-specific plans, make trade-offs within or across product lines, or influence the design and development of product-specific applications across business units. As a result, this company's key-account management devolved into a glorified administrative position, while the first company enjoyed faster sales growth.

No one should underestimate the effort required to reinforce new approaches with new metrics and performance management. Before one high-tech company could boost its returns on marketing investments, it had to rationalize hundreds of different metrics (often derived from inconsistent sources) that various product groups tracked. After agreeing on a dozen key performance indicators that would inform planning and performance management across the marketing organization, the company developed four marketing scorecards—one each at the global, regional, business unit, and product level. Each scorecard emphasized the KPIs that were most relevant to managers at that level. The regional scorecard, for example, used customer metrics (such as the penetration of retailers), while the product scorecard focused more on consumer preferences (such as satisfaction with products). A consistent set of inputs made it possible to aggregate and compare the results achieved by every product, region, and business group.

Improved tools, processes, definitions of roles, and performance management are key components of a commercial operating system. In effect, it is a blueprint for consistent, leading-edge sales and marketing in the two or three functional areas—such as pricing, brand, segment, channel, or key-account management—most closely linked to a company's strategic priorities. Such an operating system is valuable both for initiating change and for institutionalizing it. (For more details on this topic, see "The power of a commercial operating system," on page 60.)

Building capabilities

The complex and conceptual nature of marketing and sales requires companies to help their frontline professionals develop a range of tacit skills, such as making trade-offs and solving problems, rather than simply transferring "hard" knowledge. But many companies have learned through experience that formal training is woefully ineffective at building such skills. More successful approaches rely rather on apprenticeship, buttressed by basic training and part-time support, to establish new ways of working (Exhibit 2). By apprenticeship, we don't just mean training tailored to real tasks; we mean learning by doing something important for a business.

EXHIBIT 2

Learning by doing

Transforming capabilities into actions

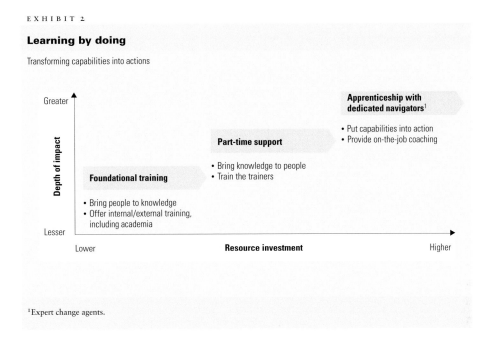

¹Expert change agents.

If people learn best by doing, someone needs to help them *do*. Much as Toyota Motor sends dozens of engineers to its partner-suppliers for as long as two years to help the suppliers learn the Toyota production system, marketing organizations need a pool of specialized, expert change agents to build skills among frontline employees and to help them engage with new systems. We call these experts *navigators*, and the way they introduce new capabilities in parallel with new systems and processes *mini-transformations*—which frequently occur first in a specific business unit, geography, or segment. Although developing a pool of navigators is resource intensive, failing to do so, we find, often leads to disappointing results.

A pharmaceutical company identified direct sales to doctors as a core skill in need of upgrading. The company chose a group of its best salespeople, who took part in a pilot program intended for rollout to the whole sales force, to serve as navigators. During the pilot, the navigators helped to shape new key-account-management processes, selling tools, and tactics checklists. After it ended, they committed more than 50 percent of their time to coaching and mentoring hundreds of salespeople in new geographies and product areas. Their status as high-performing salespeople gave them instant credibility, and their involvement in the pilot made them true believers and ideal teachers.

In contrast, a medical-device company couldn't roll out a successful pilot to other regions and business units because it failed to give its sales staff personal, on-the-job coaching or mentoring. Instead, it provided several days of training and thick binders filled with tools and processes, which went largely unused because the salespeople hadn't absorbed these systems through practical effort and didn't have coaches to help them through the tough spots. Eventually, even salespeople in the pilot business unit who changed their jobs fell back on old habits.

Mind-sets and behavior

No company should underestimate the corrosive potential of deep-seated beliefs such as "I can't lose this customer," "volume trumps margin," "if I take that risk I'll be shot down," or "the company doesn't really care about. . . ." Executives launching any change program must counteract such mind-sets and the resulting behavior. To do so, they should diagnose the underlying cultural barriers and apply a combination of hard interventions (such as changes to the incentive structure) and soft ones (like role-modeling).

But underlying assumptions are difficult to change, particularly for sales and marketing executives, who, compared with their counterparts in operations, typically have little experience with major change programs. Marketing executives may be surprised by how much effort is required to diagnose potentially counterproductive mind-sets, to begin dislodging them, and to follow up with supporting systems—from technology to compensation plans—that can convince employees of management's resolve.

The experience of a European insurance company illustrates just how many reinforcing initiatives may be needed to change mind-sets (Exhibit 3). The company sought to boost its performance by building longer-term, trust-based relationships with customers. Before launching an effort to build the relationship skills of its salespeople, it spent time interviewing and holding focus groups with them, as well as conducting more quantitative surveys. These diagnostic efforts revealed that since many employees placed great value on the immediate gratification they received from closing deals, they emphasized transactional relationships and limited their follow-up with problem customers. The company also uncovered an infrequently stated but widely held belief among the salespeople that the insurance they peddled wasn't worth its price, so that their job, in essence, was to "rip people off."

Since these beliefs ran headfirst into the goal of building trust-based relationships, changing such mind-sets was the centerpiece of the company's

EXHIBIT 3

Changing mind-sets

Initiatives to change mind-sets and behavior (disguised example of European insurance company)

I will change my behavior, if . . .

Leadership actions
Specific, meaningful actions by top team and opinion leaders

Role models
. . . I see leaders and peers walk the talk

Comprehensive communication
. . . I know what I need to change and why

Communicating change
Thematic communications—personalized and delivered interactively down to the front line—with new language and images reinforcing shifts

Personal insight
. . . I know which mind-set and personal fears stand in the way of change

New employee 'contract'
Opportunities, incentives, consequences

Reinforcing systems, processes
. . . the systems/processes support my change

Talent, skill development
. . . I have the skills to behave differently

Frontline training
Workshop and coaching on new ways of working

Revitalization workshops
Insights, skills for establishing new individual mind-sets, behavior

effort. To start, the CEO and other top executives made a series of public statements describing the attitudes they wanted salespeople to have about customer relationships. Then they began role-modeling those attitudes in meetings. Next, the company evaluated all of its salespeople according to their willingness and ability to work collaboratively with customers. The top 25 percent became change agents, and some of them helped senior managers to rewrite the call scripts that all sales reps would use. Once the company had taken these initial steps, it began rolling out the program more broadly through several other moves:

- a peer-mentoring program anchored in examples of best practice

- internal and external public commitments by senior executives to achieving the company's sales goals and to increasing the number of repeat customers and long-term relationships

- the internal publication of testimonials from customers about inter-actions with relationship-oriented salespeople

- new compensation schemes that rewarded the maintenance of longer-term relationships more generously than transactional business

Over time, the mind-sets of the company's salespeople across Europe truly did change. Operating in a mature, highly competitive industry, the company exceeded an aggressive set of targets for earnings and revenue growth.

Transformation design

Many companies, facing the complexity and freedom inherent in marketing and sales, adopt an à la carte approach to change. Rather than employing the programmatic rigor and pace of a Six Sigma or lean-operations transformation, these companies let their business units, country organizations, and districts choose from a broad menu of ideas and tools to meet their overall performance goals. In our experience, this approach is mistaken. Marketing and sales transformations require a change process with the same staging and discipline as analogous efforts in operations. Indeed, marketing's more fluid nature means that executives must devote unusually large amounts of time and effort to designing the transformation. The program must replicate across the company whatever should be consistent while giving frontline managers space where they need it. In addition, senior executives should review the program's overall progress and make trade-offs—such as how centralized or tailored to individual business units the effort should be—more frequently and in greater detail than they do for most operational-change programs.

To understand how these issues play out in practice, consider the experience of two chemical companies. The first, a single-business-unit provider of nutritional additives, suffered from vague processes and unclear accountability for most marketing and sales activities, which had historically been less important because of patent protection and cartelized competition. The second, a specialty-chemical maker that was the product of a series of mergers, comprised five divisions with 20 separate business units varying drastically in size and marketing skills.

The nutritional-chemical maker, given its simpler organizational structure, found it relatively straightforward to manage its effort centrally, to adopt top-down goals, and to use standardized approaches throughout the organization. Standardization was particularly valuable because it helped raise a broad set of marketing and sales skills from their weak starting points. To avoid having frontline professionals feel that the new approach was being imposed, the company involved many of these employees in the design of the effort to build new skills and identified a wide range of change leaders to promote them. In 12 months, it upgraded the skills of more than 500 people and, over two years, improved its return on sales (ROS) by nearly 4 percent.

For the specialty-chemical company, by contrast, a centralized change effort would have been disastrous. Because the company's divisions and business units were diverse, it needed to build its skills selectively, to develop new processes in a flexible way, and to set more targets from the bottom up. To avoid having the transformation veer out of control, the company created a small core team that moved from division to division, helping each to tailor pilot programs to its skills and needs. Over four years, this larger company rolled out new skills and approaches to more than 3,000 marketing and sales professionals, thus helping to boost its ROS by roughly 4 percent.

Although selective tailoring is usually crucial in change efforts that embrace a number of business units, many companies fail to fine-tune their approach. One diversified materials company, for example, had disappointing results when it tried to force onto Europe some new key-account-management and transaction-pricing systems that had been perfected in North America. Even when applied to products that were similar in the two regions, the new approaches were ineffective in Europe because of differences in competitors' reactions, the customers' expectations about discounting and payment terms, and the nature of relationships.

In contrast, another global materials company took extreme care in overhauling several of its skills, processes, and tools. By determining which of them could be used consistently (such as a system for calculating the SKU-to-delivery-point cost) and which would need to be modified by business unit or even by product within a given geography (such as brand-management and transaction-pricing approaches), the company laid the foundation for a successful transformation.

———

By tailoring classic change-management techniques to the specific needs of sales and marketing, executives can increase the odds of truly transforming their commercial organizations.

Joel Claret (joel_claret@mckinsey.com), **Pierre Mauger** (pierre_mauger@mckinsey.com), and **Eric Roegner** (eric_roegner@mckinsey.com) are members of McKinsey's global marketing and sales practice. Joel Claret is a director and Pierre Mauger is an associate principal in McKinsey's Geneva office; Eric Roegner is a principal in the Cleveland office.

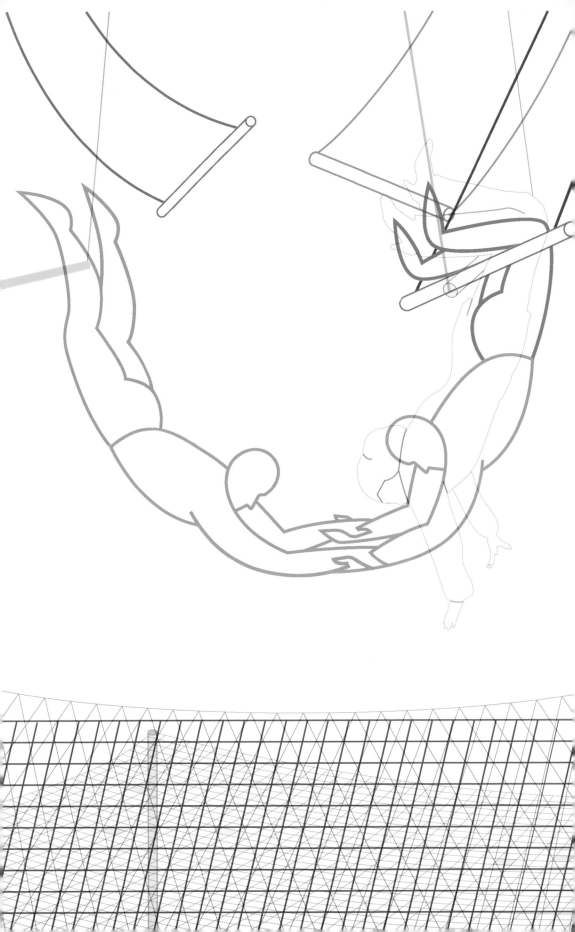

Leading change:
An interview with the
CEO of P&G

Rajat K. Gupta and Jim Wendler

Alan G. Lafley recalls vividly the market's initial disappointment when he took the helm of Procter & Gamble, in June 2000. "I remember being in the basement of the television studio here in Cincinnati at 6 PM on the day [my appointment] was announced. I was the deer in the headlights, being grilled about the company and about why it was doing so badly. And the stock price had gone down a few bucks that day because I was a total unknown." Under Lafley's predecessor, the hard-driving insider Durk Jager, the company had issued three profit warnings in four months. On one momentous day, its shares fell by a full 30 percent. No wonder investors had hoped for a more dramatic gesture, such as the appointment of a prominent outsider.

Six years later, the markets are looking at Lafley and P&G very differently. From fiscal years 2000 to 2005, the giant company's profits jumped by almost 84 percent, to $10.9 billion, and revenues increased by almost 42 percent, to nearly $57 billion. Investors have embraced P&G's future thanks to new products ranging from Swiffer (a sweeper offering for floor surfaces) to Actonel (a prescription medication for osteoporosis), as well as innovations in a wide range of established brands. And the $57.3 billion acquisition of Gillette—completed in October 2005 and by far the largest in P&G's history—has been well received by investors and analysts, who are generally skeptical about major deals.

The full story of P&G's turnaround is packed with complex, interlocking decisions about brands, personnel, technology, markets, facilities, and much else. In Lafley's view, "You can exhort all you want about excellent execution; you're not going to get it unless you have disciplined strategic choices, a structure that supports the strategy, systems that enable large organizations to work and execute together, a winning culture, and leadership that's inspirational."

The meaning of transformation

Lafley emphasizes the key difference between a true transformation and incremental business building by describing the role he played during his first 15 years with the company: "That wasn't transformation. No, the game then was: take another half a share point and another half a margin point, build to a 50 percent market share, and take 85 percent of the profits and returns that are outsized in that industry. It was very much like classical military strategy, where you just keep putting on pressure, you just keep extending the lines, you just keep rolling up the weakest competitors, and so on."

Over time, however, the desire to compete in this way can erode into complacency, which Lafley has consciously tried to avoid. "You can get used to being a player without being a winner. There's a big difference between the two. So I became interested in transforming players into winners." Once a company's culture has changed so much that being a mere player is acceptable, Lafley argues, the culture must be transformed. At that stage, just trying to improve the numbers isn't enough. Deeper change is required.

Sometimes the need for a change is obvious from a company's competitive position. Lafley recalls his years heading P&G's Asian operations: "We were the last into Asia. We were a small player there in comparison with Unilever, which had been there at the time of the Raj, and Nestlé, which had been there since 1900." In such an environment, P&G had to transform its performance just to become a serious player. But in other parts of the company—such as beauty care, which Lafley ran during the year before he became CEO—P&G's performance, though lagging, was still thought to be respectable. Lafley set out to change that view.

Achievable aspirations

Lafley argues that although aspirations should stretch a company, it is counterproductive to overpromise. "As a new CEO, I took P&G's company goals down to 4 to 6 percent top-line growth, which still required us to innovate to the tune of one to two points of new sales growth a year," as well as some market share growth and, on average, a point of growth from acquisitions. "And then I committed to stretching but achievable double-digit earnings-per-share growth." The share price went down again "because the first thing I did was to set lower, more realistic goals."

Nonetheless, these were indeed stretch goals, Lafley believes, because he had still publicly committed the company to growing faster than it had in recent years and faster than the industry as well. Moreover, he and his leadership team set internal goals higher than those announced externally.

Lafley reined in the company's aspirations in a second, more subtle way: he defined what he calls "the core"—core markets, categories, brands, technologies, and capabilities—and focused his near-term efforts entirely on that. P&G's markets and operations, he determined, were too vast and diverse to be turned around all at once. This decision meant, among other things, that only a fraction of the more than 100 countries where P&G operates would receive significant attention initially. "So we called out ten priority countries, and people said, 'Oh, I'm not on the list.' I just told them, 'Just keep doing a good job where you are.'"

Alan G. Lafley

Vital statistics
• Born on June 13, 1947, in Keene, New Hampshire

Education
• Graduated in 1969 with BA in history from Hamilton College
• Graduated in 1977 with MBA from Harvard Business School

Career highlights
• P&G (1977–present)
  – Chairman of the board, president, and chief executive (2002–present)
  – President and chief executive (2000–02)
  – President, global beauty care and North American market development (1999–2000)
  – Executive vice president, P&G; president, P&G North America (1998–99)
  – Executive vice president, P&G; president, P&G Asia (1995–98)
  – Group vice president, P&G; president, P&G Far East (1994–95)
  – Group vice president, P&G; president, laundry and cleaning products, P&G USA (1992–94)

Fast facts
• Served in the US Navy (1970–75)
• Serves on board of directors of numerous institutions and companies, including GE, United Negro College Fund, Hamilton College, Business Council, Business Roundtable
• Served on board of directors of GM
• Member of Harvard Club of Cincinnati

While management literature has emphasized the necessity of defining the core, Lafley underscores the importance of actually communicating the definition clearly. Indeed, he says that the need to communicate at a Sesame Street level of simplicity was one of his most important discoveries as CEO:

"So if I'd stopped at 'We're going to refocus on the company's core businesses,' that wouldn't have been good enough. The core businesses are one, two, three, four. Fabric care, baby care, feminine care, and hair care. And then you get questions: 'Well, I'm in home care. Is that a core business?' 'No.' 'What does it have to do to become a core business?' 'It has to be global leader in its industry. It has to have the best structural economics in its industry. It has to be able to grow consistently at a certain rate. It has to be able to deliver a certain cash flow return on investment.' So then business leaders understand what it takes to become a core business."

Why is such excruciating repetition and clarity required? After all, as Lafley proudly notes, P&G attracts the best and brightest from the world's finest universities. One obvious reason is the sheer scale and diversity of the workforce. The company's 100,000 people come from more than 100 cultures, and for many of them English is a second language.

Another reason is the need to unclutter the thinking of employees so that they can focus on the critical business of problem solving. "They have so many things going on in the operation of their daily businesses that they don't always take the time to stop, think, and internalize. They have to figure out what it all really means because I cannot call out the strategy for a business. I want them to use the same basic model and the same discipline to make the right choices for, say, the Philippines," where P&G has a half-billion-dollar business—a sizable operation but only 1 percent of the whole. "I want the manager there to think very consciously about what kind of culture is going to be a winner, what kind of capabilities are needed, and so on."

Coaching and coaxing

So Lafley insists that he can't babysit the businesses: to a large degree they must define their own future, while he plays the role of coach. But coaching at P&G doesn't mean coddling. On the contrary, Lafley demands that his managers take on the responsibility of making tough strategic choices. "Most human beings and most companies don't like to make choices. And they particularly don't like to make a few choices that they really have to live with. They argue, 'It's much better to have lots of options, right?'"

Those extraneous options have a way of reappearing on the table after they have been dismissed. Lafley therefore insists on a "not-do list" as an end product of the strategy process. "For example, when we chose our corporate-innovation programs, we cleared the deck of a lot of other stuff that we were then doing. So we'd have a list of all the things that we're not going to do. And if we caught people doing stuff that we said we were not going to do, we would pull the budget and the people and get them refocused on what we said we were going to do."

To help managers make these strategic choices, leaders must sometimes challenge deeply held assumptions. Lafley recalls a first meeting with his cosmetics managers in Japan after he took over Asian operations. He was known around the company for his work with the Tide brand, "so this guy said, 'You know, this is nothing like laundry detergent,' and smiled." Lafley spent much of the next month talking with consumers at sales counters and in their homes and then reported back to his team, "Do you know what I've learned after 30 days? Cosmetics is everything like laundry detergent! You need to know who your consumers are—intimately. You need to understand not just their habits and practices but their needs and wants, including those they can't articulate. Then you've got to delight them with your brands and your products." Lafley was determined not to allow the mystique of cosmetics to prevent the team from adopting classic P&G practices that had built the company and were fully applicable. A significant result of this process was the decision to promote the SK-II skin care line, which became one of the company's most successful in recent years.

Act as a role model

Being a role model is of course especially important when a CEO makes tough demands on managers. P&G's managers expect Lafley not only to make the same kinds of strategic choices he requires of them but also to act consistently on those choices. Lafley therefore recognizes that he must be ready for moments of truth that can alert the organization to his own deep commitment to P&G's aspirations.

Such moments came early in Lafley's tenure. He had to decide whether to go ahead with strong marketing support for the launch of several new brands (Actonel and Torengos in the United States, and Iams in Europe). "Profit pressure was severe. We had just missed earnings two quarters in a row, and the new brands would need strong, sustained support because they were going up against market-leading competitors. But innovation is P&G's

lifeblood, and the businesses believed in their products—all of which tested better than those of competitors—and in their brands. So we locked arms and we went ahead. When I look back now on those early weeks, it's clear that I had to make choices like these to convince P&G managers we were going to go for winning."

One of the classic problems facing any CEO during a turnaround is the possibility that managers and employees become so overwhelmed by the breadth of the changes facing them that they can't achieve any change at all. The organization freezes, as though in shock. Lafley, after all, had taken over a 163-year-old company that was accustomed to leadership in most of its markets and had been famous for its cultural pride and self-confidence. "Then all of a sudden," he notes, "all that had been shattered." Although this slump wasn't P&G's worst in living memory—that came from 1984 to 1985, when the company's earnings dipped below those of the previous 12 months for the first time in many years—it was perceived by outsiders as the worst. "Because of the role of the press, it was a more public failure."

Yet Lafley realized that P&G, though struggling, was in better shape than press reports suggested. In particular, he recognized that the company's culture, far from being a hindrance, was an asset that could be leveraged in a transformation. So he reversed his predecessor's sharp critique of the culture and affirmed its competitive value in discussions with managers and employees across the company.

"I started with P&G values and said, 'Here's what's not going to change. This is our purpose: to improve the everyday lives of people around the world with P&G brands and products that deliver better performance, quality, and value. That's not going to change. The value system—integrity, trust, ownership, leadership, and a passion for service and winning: not going to change. The six guiding principles, respect for the individual, and so on: not going to change. OK, so here's the stuff that will change. Any business that doesn't have a strategy is going to develop one; any business that has a strategy that's not winning in the marketplace is either going to change its strategy or improve its execution.' And so on. So I was very clear about what was safe and what wasn't."

This reassurance, like the intensive coaching about strategic choice and its consequences, helped the company raise its sights again.

Keep innovating

Ultimately, aspirations are energizing only when they are grounded in new ideas that can help a company win in the marketplace. Successful transformations always have a strong content dimension—particularly, of course, at companies such as P&G, where constant product innovation is a central element of strategy. Lafley, however, believed that the pendulum had swung too far toward technology during the heady new-economy years. At one point, the annual budget for "skunk works" technology—experimental projects outside the mainstream businesses—had reached $200 million. "We were spending more than tech companies were on this kind of stuff," he observes. Thus P&G, which business schools treated as the classic example of a company that builds all of its processes around consumer "pull," was now "pushing" technology into the market. This approach was certainly one way to develop new ideas, but not necessarily winning ideas.

Durk Jager had excited P&G people with these investments. Lafley describes that approach as "forward to the future," which he contrasts with his own "back to the future" mind-set: "I wanted to put consumers front and center and get back to asking, 'Who are they and what do they want?' Find out what they want and give it to them. Delight them with P&G products. So I have this incredibly simple saying: 'The consumer is the boss.' And there are two moments of truth—when consumers make their purchase decision, and when they use the product. If they're delighted at the second moment of truth, they'll repurchase our brands and hopefully begin to use our products regularly."

When Jager left the company, news accounts cited his global reorganization as a major contributor to his departure. Lafley, however, not only supported the reorganization but had also served on the team that designed it. Rather than abandon Jager's new organizational structure, Lafley used it to support his own theme of returning to a stronger consumer orientation. The new market-development operations were charged with winning the first moment of truth, the new global business units with winning the second. The new structure, says Lafley, "had a simple reason for being," and another apparent liability became an asset for the transformation.

More generally, Lafley strongly credits Jager with moving P&G toward a more external focus. Jager had begun to promote what the company calls "connect and develop"—that is, the pursuit of more externally sourced innovation. Currently, 25 percent of new products and technologies come from outside the company, but Lafley wants to raise that to 50 percent, so that "half would come out of P&G labs and half would come through P&G labs, from the outside."

Lafley is pushing for more exposure to the outside world in other ways as well—for example, by establishing strong relationships with external designers, distributing product development around the world to increase what P&G calls "consumer sensing," and even bringing John Osher, who invented the Crest SpinBrush electric rotating toothbrush, inside the company for a period to help spur innovation. All of these moves have increased the flow of new ideas.

That flow should surge again with P&G's acquisition of Gillette. Like most major deals, this one is intended to create value in a number of ways, including relatively straightforward cost efficiencies. Lafley has concrete ideas for strengthening Gillette's brands too. He believes that increased innovation will be the most significant factor in the longer run, though he concedes that it is difficult to predict, at this early stage, exactly what form innovation will take:

"My aspiration is that this deal will accelerate the growth and development of our company by a decade or two. It's clear that Gillette and P&G are two of the strongest innovators in consumer products. Gillette's a company, like us, built on innovation in their core businesses. So I'm hopeful that we'll learn a lot from each other. They're mechanical engineers, we're chemical engineers. I'm very hopeful that this combination will open up new businesses to us. If you put mechanical and chemical engineers together, they're going to see things that we don't see today, because our view of the world is bounded."

Leadership and learning

Lafley clearly has strong faith in the transformative power of learning—a faith evident not only in his aspirations for the Gillette deal but also in the coaching role he regularly assumes with managers. It is clear, as well, in his initiatives to expand P&G's formal management and leadership training: for example, he founded the company's college for general managers and teaches leadership.

His coaching role has also shown him the importance of his own learning experiences. The first months after Lafley's appointment as CEO were particularly difficult in this respect: although he had experience selling the full range of P&G products during his stint as leader of the North American market-development operation, he lacked a deep understanding of about half of the company's businesses. Some things he learned during this period were bracing: "I discovered that the cupboard was bare on the technology side in one business, that we didn't have the leadership we needed in another business, and that we didn't know what the strategy was going to be in a third business." He was learning, in effect, what was needed to coach the organization.

Although Lafley needed a period of crash learning as CEO despite his 25 years as a P&G operating manager, he credits his experience with giving him insights into ways of transforming the company. "You need to understand how to enroll a leadership team and then an organization, how to operationalize the strategy, how to get the accountability that you want all the way down the organization. The more deeply you understand something, the more willing you are to take risks and the more intelligent those risks are." His deep knowledge of the company, he says, "meant I knew how and when we could take risks and stretch ourselves to go for peak performance— without breaking down."

Does a radical change agent lie behind the cultural conservatism? Lafley paused at the "radical" label because, at least until the Gillette deal, the transformation had been the cumulative effect of a series of small, interlocking changes. No single dramatic event during the past five years defines the period, just as no evocative vision statement served as its road map. "I guess I'm a serial change agent," Lafley says.

Rajat Gupta (rajat_gupta@mckinsey.com) is a director in McKinsey's Stamford office, and **Jim Wendler** (jim_wendler@mckinsey.com) is an alumnus of the London office and an adviser to the firm.